Common Sense About Uncommon Wisdom

Common Sense About Uncommon Wisdom
Ancient Teachings of Vedanta

Dhruv S. Kaji

The Himalayan Institute Press
Honesdale, Pennsylvania

Published by:
The Himalayan Institute Press
RR 1, Box 405
Honesdale, Pennsylvania 18431

First Printing

Cover design by Michele Wetherbee
Page design by Joan Gazdik Gillner

The paper used in this publication meets the minimum requirements of American National Standard for Information Sciences—Permanence of Paper for Printed Library Materials, ANSI Z39.48-1984.

Library of Congress Cataloging-in-Publication Data

Kaji, Dhruv S., 1951-
    Common sense about uncommon wisdom : ancient teachings of Vedanta / Dhruv S. Kaji.
        p. cm.
    Rev. ed. of: Yet another book on Vedanta, 1999.
    Includes bibliographical references.
    ISBN 0-89389-192-4 (paperback : alk. paper)
    1. Vedanta. I. Kaji, Dhruv S., 1951- Yet another book on Vedanta. II. Title.

B132.V3 K25 2001
181'.48--dc21   00-050562

Contents

◆

Preface

◆

IT HAS BEEN TWO YEARS since I completed the manuscript for the first version of this book, which was published in India under the title *Yet Another Book on Vedanta*. I am delighted and gratified that the Himalayan Institute Press in the United States has now decided to publish an international edition.

I have used this opportunity to carry out several small but important revisions in the text and to incorporate valuable suggestions which I have received from readers. Some portions have also been modified to make the text easier to read and understand.

As I continue my study of Vedanta, I am struck again and again by the beauty and relevance of its teachings. I sincerely hope that a book such as this will help some of its readers on their personal voyage of discovery.

Introductory Note

◆

LIKE SO MANY MAJOR EVENTS in life which form a watershed only in retrospect, I was introduced to the timeless wisdom called Vedanta some years ago by happy accident. There was no particular plan to genuinely expose myself to the teachings of Vedanta at that time. I also had no inkling about the impact that this body of ancient knowledge was going to have on my thinking, values, and objectives. In fact, like many others in our age of logic and technology, I initially approached Vedanta with deep suspicion. This attitude seemed entirely reasonable for something which I assumed combined an ancient (and apparently irrelevant) religion along with some incredible metaphysical speculation. My initial thrust was more of an intellectual game to confirm the facile prejudgment that Vedanta could only be one more sop for the weak or the mindless.

Such a shaky and unpromising start marked the opening of an immensely enjoyable and fulfilling period in my life. In my Vedantic journey so far, I have met some very wise and kind people; I have been moved to childlike wonder as well as to occasional tears by the profundity and sublimity of thoughts and experiences contained in these teachings; I have also learnt more about life and my own self here than through any other pursuit.

Startlingly and fortunately, even my preliminary exploration so far has had the effect of transforming my suspicions and misconceptions into awe and reverence. A miracle of meaning and hope together with gratitude and humility is gradually but definitely conquering places within me previously ruled by fear and by lack of meaning. A growing sense of peace and well-being is beginning to replace the frantic activity, cynicism, and acquisitiveness which had almost unknowingly become an integral part of my approach to life. I now look forward to deeper exploration and further learning as well as to personal practice and assimilation; unless I am able to do this, these teachings will remain hollow concepts which will fade without delivering their full and permanent effects.

The path of getting even to this early stage has, on several occasions, been full of doubt, pain, and frustration. There have been times when there has been desperate need for some rational framework and well-defined process within which apparently random and often contradictory statements could be fitted. Difficulties in finding clear answers to issues which seemed to hopelessly knot up the intellect as well as emotions have led to both rage and despondency.

Despite such initial difficulties in approaching Vedanta, it seems to me that for more and more of us there is an increased longing to understand and feel a wider context within which we can experience ourselves as an integral part of creation and not just as its conquerors and exploiters. However, our relentless and one-sided pursuit of the rational-scientific way of viewing everything has caused us to concentrate on quick and finite answers which can comfortably fit within ready-made niches in our conditioned intellects. While our current abilities perform better than ever in initiating and accelerating changes in all spheres of living, we forget that the faster the rushing stream of events, the greater becomes our need to find firm ground. After all, as it has been true in all the past millennia, the fact remains that all life is subject to change as well as ultimate dissolution and that a part of each individual through all ages is in quest of something immutable and imperishable. Vedanta deals with this need by teaching us a different way of thinking and by exposing us to a different kind of knowledge, both of which lead to an all-encompassing perspective and a new level of understanding. From this vantage point, the conflict between the mystical and the scientific ways of thinking is resolved in a higher awareness in which all thoughts have their source.

However, to get started on this much-needed path of knowledge contained in Vedanta, it is first necessary to demystify this ancient wisdom and remove many of the false notions and prejudices which have grown over the centuries to encrust and hide the beauty, vitality, and relevance of its perennial truths. The purpose of this book, then, is not to get very much into its detailed teachings (for which I am not qualified in any case) but to share some insights into Vedanta's general structure and develop a useful approach to its great truths. This may be of some help to persons in our modern times who may want to explore this mystical and translogical knowledge without completely giving up the use of logic or the use of explicit process within a well-defined structure; after all, these are the tools we all use, often and well, in obtaining and interpreting knowledge in other fields. My views and insights are, of course, subjective and all their aspects cannot have general acceptance. It is only hoped that for those people who share my personal conditioning and mindset, this introductory book will provide a clear preview in a modern perspective and thereby add some joy (or remove some frustration) in the process of exploring Vedanta. In addition, this book may also give a glimpse of what the committed study of Vedanta entails for the serious student.

Lastly, from personal experience I am acutely aware of the limitations of any book on this subject in communicating even a touch of the true spirit of Vedanta. By attempting to bring some clarity and clearing some of the dense forest of misconceptions surrounding this fundamental knowledge,

I only hope that you will be encouraged to pursue Vedanta with the help of a proper teacher. We must always keep in mind the fact that no actual learning is possible here without a true teacher and to find one is tremendous fortune in itself.

I do hope that apart from gleaning some useful information from this book, you will also enjoy yourself as you read. With this in mind, I have deliberately kept the tone of writing somewhat light and conversational. This is in no way to downplay the exalted and revered wisdom of Vedanta. I do not believe that the only way to show reverence is to be somber. I also believe that any great truth should be simple in its essence and that the process of its discovery need not exclude joy. In fact, if we pursue Vedanta in the proper manner and give its teachings a chance to work on us, we should find greater zest for life and also find good humor and laughter coming more readily to us.

Chapter One

◆

What Is Vedanta?

AS VEDANTA IS THE subject of this entire book, it is important to be clear about its meaning at the outset. In essence, Vedanta is the unique means of knowledge for resolving the fundamental and universal ignorance about our own true nature. All human beings are born with this ignorance. As this ignorance is about our own nature and as our true nature (whatever it may be!) is the very substratum of our own experiences, emotions, thoughts, and actions, there is no aspect of our lives which is unaffected by this fundamental ignorance. Growth and objectivity are always compromised by ignorance. Because Vedanta deals with fundamental self-ignorance, it is the path of ultimate human growth and the means of fulfilling a human being's highest potential. However, this sort of meaning is putting the cart before the horse and is not particularly helpful at this stage. Let us, therefore, begin with the simple and literal meaning of the word *Vedanta*.

The word *Vedanta* is from the ancient Indian language of Sanskrit. This word is actually a compound of two other words: *veda* and *antah*. *Veda* literally means a compilation of that which is known[1] and is used to refer to a body of very ancient knowledge spread over four large and famous compilations known as the *Rig Veda*, the *Yajur Veda*, the *Sama Veda*, and the *Atharva Veda*. These four compilations contain invocations, prayers, detailed rituals, and philosophical thoughts and insights. The philosophical portions are found in the last section (or at the end) of each of the four compilations of the Vedas. The word *antah* merely means *end* and so the word *Vedanta* (by combining *veda* and *antah*) refers to that body of knowledge which is to be found at the end of the Vedas. It is just a locational meaning. Used in this sense, the word *Vedanta* is synonymous with the word *Upanishads*, which, despite a different etymological meaning, refers to the same body of knowledge.

The philosophical thoughts and insights at the end of each of the four Vedas can be broken down into several independent portions, with each one being characterized by a different style of writing, or a different approach designed to highlight a different facet of the same great wisdom. Each of these separate portions has been traditionally referred to as a particular Upanishad. Thus we have, for instance, the *Isha Upanishad* (from the *Yajur Veda*), the *Kena Upanishad* (from the *Sama Veda*), the *Mandukya Upanishad* (from the *Atharva Veda*), the *Aitreya Upanishad* (from the *Rig Veda*), and so on. All the Upanishads deal with the same subject but each individual Upanishad can stand on its own. Nobody quite knows how many Upanishads actually existed once upon a time because many have been destroyed and lost forever. This is not surprising, because originally the individual Upanishads (and, indeed, the entire Vedas) were passed on by people who memorized them by listening to their teachers. They, in turn, got their

---

1. The word *veda* in turn can be related further back to its root *vid*, which means to *know*. It is interesting to note the similarity between the Sanskrit word *vid* (to know) and the Latin word *video* (I see); to see something is a way of knowing it.

own students to memorize them, and this went on down the generations. Committing them to writing began much later—and that too in the form of words scratched onto dried palm leaves, which had to face the problems of fire, floods, pests, and perhaps even hungry goats! What is surprising is that we seem to have about 120 Upanishads available to us even now. Of the available Upanishads, 10 are often referred to as the principal Upanishads, not because they are very different from all the other Upanishads but because the great eighth-century teacher Shankara chose to write a commentary on them.

Incidentally, scholars fix the date of the Vedas over a large range of time, going back to anywhere between two thousand years to four thousand years ago, and there are no named or known authors for these magnificent collections of telling and writing; Indian tradition terms the knowledge of the Vedas as *apaurusheya* and *anadi*, which mean, respectively, *not created by any human being* and *timeless*. We, however, need not initially get into such aspects or controversies to use and to benefit from Vedanta.

Let us now come back to the wider meaning of the word *Vedanta*, which is also used to refer to one out of the six traditional Indian schools of philosophy.[2] *Vedanta* here refers to a whole school of philosophy, which accepts the authority of the Vedas with special emphasis on the Upanishads portion. Apart from the actual contents of the Upanishads, *Vedanta* when used to refer to this integrated philosophical structure includes widely varying views of great sages[3] and an established teaching tradition. It is interesting to note that the famous *Bhagavad Gita* is not part of Vedanta as an actual portion of the Vedas (because it is not contained in any part of the Vedas) but is considered by all to

---

2. The other five schools are *sankhya*, *yoga*, *nyaya*, *vaisheshika*, and *mimamsa*.
3. The three most important views included in Vedanta are the *advaita* view of Shankara, the *vishishta advaita* view of Ramanuja, and the *dvaita* view of Madhva.

be one of the most important treatises of Vedanta philosophy.

For the purpose of this book and in order to avoid confusion, I will now use the term *Upanishads* when referring to the actual contents of the last section of the Vedas, and the term *Vedanta* when referring to the entire school of thought and teaching known by the same name. Lastly, when I use the term *Vedanta* I will be restricting myself only to the *advaita* doctrine of Shankara, which is the oldest and the most commonly accepted doctrine within Vedanta.

The *advaita* Vedanta of Shankara means the *non-dual* Vedanta of Shankara.[4] Why can we not say *single* instead of *non-dual?* In common parlance we could do so and this would not make much difference, but here the term *non-dual* is deliberately used to remove even the slightest possibility of duality which the word *single* may convey. For instance, the term *single* could be understood as something which could be broken down into parts (such as two halves), or the concept of *single* as *one* could be seen as part of a set consisting of one, two, three, four, and so on. So, when the word *advaita* is used, the idea is to communicate a sense of a total unity which does not admit the possibility of any duality. We can therefore conclude that advaita Vedanta deals with a philosophy centered around a unity so great, so complete, so basic that all duality is ruled out. What this great unity is all about forms part of the core teachings of Vedanta, which we will briefly look into only in a later chapter.

I realize that the foregoing setting out of the meaning or definition of a few Sanskrit words may seem tedious and unnecessary, but as Vedanta can use only the resources of words in order to attempt to convey its subtle message, it is more than usually important to settle precise word meanings.

---

4. The word *advaita* comes from the Sanskrit word *dvaita* and the prefix *a*. *Dvaita* means *two* or *dual* and the prefix *a* means *not* in the sense of negation. So, *advaita* means *not two* or *non-dual*.

We also have to clearly understand the connotations of the word *philosophy* when we label advaita Vedanta as a philosophy. Philosophy means the pursuit of wisdom and knowledge; this pursuit need not have any personal value except the inclination towards establishing an abstract truth for the truth's sake. The pursuit of Vedanta is quite different: here the pursuit of truth is not an end in itself; nor is the truth which is being pursued just any other truth. Vedanta is the study of the true nature of humankind (and the true nature of all creation) with the objective of resolving the fundamental self-ignorance with which all human beings are born. This natural ignorance leads to a universal sense of limitation and lacking in each one of us.

Following a logical process and using the experiences of our everyday living as its basis, Vedanta analyzes any individual's usual conclusion of being subject to several limitations; such a conclusion arises naturally from the fact that the human body and mind are limited in terms of time, space, knowledge, and happiness. Vedanta then looks into the universal response of every human being to this notion of limitation by attempting to become different (healthier body, sharper intellect, and pleasanter emotions—or, in other words, longer life, better knowledge, and more happiness). This analysis ends with the very clear conclusion that the *final end* to the basic sense of lacking in any human being can never come from attempts to work on the body, the intellect, or the emotions. This is because all human attempts are limited or finite and because any effort means a cost in terms of something expended or something else forgone. The only possible solution can come from the knowledge that the limitations of our body and mind do not actually affect us because our true nature is different.

This knowledge is not the ordinary knowledge of outside objects or the knowledge of means and ends that we use to achieve our usual plans. This is knowledge of our own true self or knowledge of that knower within us for whom even our body and mind are just known objects. It is actually knowledge of that ultimate subject within us which we refer to by the pronoun *I*.

As the subject of our study and investigation in Vedanta is the real *I* and this *I* is the basis of all our observations and experiences (*I* see, *I* hear, *I* love, *I* hate, *I* am happy, *I* am upset . . .), it is impossible to have that *I* available to us as an object for our observation and examination. In some ways this is similar to the fact that it is also impossible for our eyes to see themselves. However, we can use a mirror to observe our eyes, and the teachings of Vedanta are really a word-mirror which, when used by a proper and competent teacher with an adequately prepared student, would result in the removal of ignorance surrounding that *I*. The removal of this ignorance is an achievement which brings dramatic results for the student by changing their entire orientation. Vedanta then proceeds to examine the nature of the rest of creation perceived by each *I* and establishes the identity between the *I*, the rest of creation, and the creator. It further goes on to the only reality which is beyond the creator. In doing all this, Vedanta really operates as a unique means of knowledge (called *pramana* in Sanskrit), much as the eye is the unique means of knowledge of forms and color. As a unique means for the knowledge of one's own self, Vedanta can never be fully substituted by any other means of knowledge, just as the ears or any other sense can never fully substitute for eyesight.

As we said at the outset, we are not going to get into the detailed teachings of Vedanta to attempt to see ourselves and our surroundings as reflected in the mirror of Vedanta. All we need to know at present is that Vedanta establishes the fundamental human problem (of a constant sense of limitation and lacking) which is unchanged over time and location, proposes a special kind of knowledge as the only solution, and then holds itself out as the appropriate means of obtaining that knowledge. If Vedanta does, in fact, live up to its promise, then it cannot be treated as just one of the many schools of philosophy; it must merit special consideration because of its basic and far-reaching importance.

Incidentally, it is perfectly normal at this stage if one is not clear about the real significance of the word *advaita* or has difficulty in understanding what is meant by *the real I* or does not fully appreciate the nature of *the fundamental human problem*. The attempt so far has been only to introduce these terms and concepts. Some of them will become clearer as this book progresses and others will be deliberately not explored deeply because they are of such subtlety and importance that the task of unfolding their full meaning has to be left to an appropriate teacher.

However, you could be asking yourself some more preliminary questions at this point, which may make you feel uncomfortable or bring a sense of futility about reading any further. These sorts of doubts and feelings need some addressing at the outset. So let us look at some of these hypothetical but possible issues.

Let us begin with a person who feels that all this Vedanta business may be relevant only to a troubled or tortured individual who has abnormal problems or who has abnormal difficulty in dealing with even normal problems. This person may say, "I have no particular difficulty in dealing with life; I do not suffer from this so-called fundamental human problem which Vedanta is supposed to deal with. I have a loving and happy family; I enjoy my work and look forward to sports, music, and vacations. Once in a while all areas of life present a problem, which I can usually fix, and I have no great difficulty in accepting the few that I cannot. I do not really need Vedanta." To such persons (who actually form the majority of those for whom life has been reasonably fortunate) I would say that it is not the purpose of Vedanta to introduce some disquiet or raise the bogey of a problem which does not exist for them. As we saw a little earlier, Vedanta is not the pursuit of an abstract notion or the dissection of some scholarly problem—it is relevant only if it has the potential of working for us in our lives as they are now by adding something of direct value or by removing some real problem. If we find that Vedanta cannot add any value to us then we should certainly not waste any time in this pursuit unless we wish to do so as a matter of curiosity or for casual information. Further, if we should run into anyone who speaks the words of Vedanta but whose objective is to make us feel ignorant or crass merely because we are not willing to plunge headlong into the pursuit of Vedanta, then we would do well to give that person a wide berth in this matter. Having said this, let me then go on to say that Vedanta is a resource at least for times when problems and troubles do visit our lives.

While we all hope and work for relatively trouble-free lives (and some of us do seem to go through life without any major upheavals), once in a while stock markets do crash, businesses do collapse, children turn out to be contrary to our dreams, spouses get estranged, and, for all of us, old age and the prospect of death do catch up. Further, even without any major external event, our minds go through lows, doubts, insecurities, and fears. It is in these times that Vedanta comes into its own. It seems nothing more than prudent to examine Vedanta's capability in helping us to deal with unfortunate or unpleasant events and with the pain caused by certain changes in the state of the mind.

Let me also add one other thought on this subject. In the process of building up understanding about the true nature of the world and ourselves, Vedanta goes into a brilliant analysis of human needs and the basis for all human actions. The insights and clarity brought about by this analysis are truly wonderful. They are as relevant today as they were in ancient times because fundamental human nature has not changed. Just a little clearer and more objective understanding of why and how we and others around us act helps a great deal in managing our own internal drives and relating better with others. This alone, to my mind, justifies some pursuit of Vedanta. At this juncture I must clarify that I am saying this only to meet some initial doubts; Vedanta is so fundamental, so complete, and so magnificent that to reduce it to some clever tricks to improve our relationships or to aid our careers is like using the blaze of the sun where the flickering light of a candle is enough.

Let us turn to another type of person who may feel that the pursuit of Vedanta could be a very rewarding exercise—but not just yet. This person may think, "At this stage of life I need to build my career and my security; I have responsibilities to my family; I also want to enjoy myself. I am not particularly curious to know any 'real I' and I am not really concerned about the nature of creation and its creator. Perhaps when my work is more or less done and when I am peacefully basking in the glow of the setting sun in the evening of my life, I might like to expose myself to teachings such as Vedanta. But, no thank you, not right now!" Here again, it would be wrong to try to put some kind of complex into this person because they think that Vedanta is not for them at present. The fact is that all persons at all times are already on a path which ultimately points to Vedanta. All human pursuits and activities are based on removing some form of perceived limitation and, therefore, are attempts to become something different. Money is sought to remove a sense of insecurity or to gain an ability to do things which are presently beyond our reach; a personal relationship is sought and nurtured to seek emotional fulfillment needed to fill a void in this area;

a movie is watched to pleasantly pass some time in a situation where boredom would have kept us from feeling good. Vedanta looks at the whole range of our pursuits and classifies them into sensible categories. It then logically leads us to the conclusion that all these pursuits, no matter how successful, cannot keep the fundamental sense of limitation at bay for long. This effectively makes us *perpetual seekers* (of security, love, entertainment, longevity, you name it).

Vedanta deals with this seeking not by saying that seeking is wrong but by leading us to discover the fundamental reality behind ourselves, as a result of which all our seeking falls into its correct perspective. After Vedanta's teachings, the usual seeking can still superficially continue but the actual results of such seeking are now stripped of their capacity to become the sole determinants of our happiness.

But to consciously turn to Vedanta seems to require, for most of us, a certain amount of preparation by the pursuit of the usual objectives (preferably with a good measure of success in achieving those objectives). Then, one fine day, faint new thoughts start stirring in our mind—thoughts that the commonly followed game plan of obtaining and retaining happiness does not seem to be fully delivering its promise; that the usual approach seems to imply remaining a permanent seeker; that the solution to this state may be other than striving harder for the same old objectives or beyond picking up yet another objective from the collection of usual objectives. This type of thinking, however faint and tentative, is a major break with past conditioning and is the first step in the Vedantic journey of discovering a new level of objectives and a completely different approach.

In a way, all our pursuits slowly but inexorably take us closer to the point where the discovery of Vedanta becomes inevitable and are part of the Vedantic journey, even if we may not recognize or acknowledge this. A quest for a more fundamental and different objective is only a matter of time and, therefore, there is no particular need to worry if Vedanta does not seem to be relevant to someone right now. Virtually all of us initially try to push away Vedanta's knowledge because we intuitively know that this will cause a paradigm shift in our pattern of thinking. We tell ourselves that eternal seeking is the very basis of life and that it is something which we enjoy forever! There is obvious comfort and security in conforming and in sticking to the familiar. There is also natural reluctance in even thinking of the possibility that the years of effort and concerns in a particular direction could have been somewhat misdirected. It seems simpler to let our hopes keep on conquering our actual experiences of life and carry on till something spontaneously gives way within us. Then the state of being continuous seekers suddenly becomes irksome and we begin to reexamine our superstructure of habits and conditioning.

It is difficult to predict when that first questioning of the basis of the usual game plan of living will happen in a specific individual's case. Luck certainly seems to have a lot to do with this. As we cannot order good fortune on demand, one of the things we can do is to be a bit more selective in the reading that we do and in the company that we keep. Further, what is even more important is for us to make a conscious attempt to be more aware of our own life's experiences in terms of our desires and our actions as well as the nature and duration of the consequent happiness or unhappiness. There is a wealth of knowledge to be gained by just occasionally pausing to take stock and reflecting on our own doings.

Let us look at one last type of reaction when Vedanta is being talked about. Here we have a person who may say, "I of course know that there is more to life than seeking security and pleasure. I have firm belief in a just and almighty God. I try to always act in consonance with God's law as I and my religion see it. The culmination of my life would be to find a place in God's domain where I could continue to serve him and bask under his benign gaze." Once again, if someone is satisfied with the meaning and purpose that their religion and their concept of God provide them with, they should certainly not let anyone undermine this. However, for some of us there is an almost overpowering urge to know more about the mystery of creation, the reality of the creator, and of the riddle of life, its purpose and its end. Unfortunately, usual philosophies do not seem to go far enough to provide answers which will satisfy both the intellect and emotions; religions and theologies seem to stop at a notion of God who himself has no explanation or higher purpose. If we need to have some greater meaning to life beyond the tangible or the ephemeral, then we need to find our lives meaningful in a larger perspective. But we can then question that larger perspective in the same way.

For example, if our individual lives have greater meaning because of their role in our families, then one may question the significance and purpose of our families in the grand scheme of things. If families have a meaning only in the context of the community, we can ask what makes communities important or relevant. And one can do this with cities, nations, and the entirety of humankind. If, at the end of this, we are going to be told that everything has meaning and relevance because of God, why can we not ask the same question about God? Why must we accept God as an end in himself? This is where many ethical and theological streams seem to lose their way in the sands of shaky ideals and dogma. This is where Vedanta begins. This is the point we come to when we have had enough of being continuous seekers and after we have tried to resolve some fundamental questions via other philosophies and religion.

Chapter Two

♦

What Vedanta Is Not

IN MY PERSONAL QUEST to learn something from Vedanta, I continue to be surprised by the sheer number of misconceptions and false notions which I seem to have acquired from my surroundings as well as from my own thinking. In the process of learning I have had to make greater and more painful effort in unlearning than in imbibing something really new. This struggle is, of course, an integral part of the learning process. However, to have some idea of the more common of these false notions would be helpful at least at the initial stage. What is even more important is that if these misunderstandings are not cleared up, some of them may form the basis for prejudging and rejecting Vedanta without actually understanding its true nature. We are therefore going to devote this chapter to looking at some of the more usual misunderstandings and prejudices which surround this subject. (If you have had no prior exposure to Vedanta, then of course you cannot have any specific misconceptions about it. Even if this is so, I think that this chapter may yet be interesting and useful because most of us harbor some notions—

usually uncomfortable!—about matters in the realm of the metaphysical and mystical.)

We should remember that questions about human existence and significance are perennial and universal. There is no human being to whom these questions do not occur in some form at some time. The seductive strength of Vedanta lies in the promise that it will provide answers to such questions. However, there is also parallel trepidation in approaching the issues that Vedanta raises, coupled with some intimidation by its terminology. A number of misconceptions about Vedanta stem from this conflict. Lack of faith that there really *could* be any answers is another basis for wrong notions. And of course there is nothing better than ignorance or prejudice as a source of false ideas on any subject!

As we saw in the last chapter, Vedanta is purely and simply a direct means of knowledge. The knowledge here, of course, is special because it is not the usual kind of knowledge of objects, processes, or concepts, but knowledge of the knower; this special knowledge needs a unique means by which it becomes known. Vedanta is that means (just as hearing is the direct and unique means of the knowledge of sound). Any notion attributed to Vedanta which is not in keeping with its nature as a means of knowledge is likely to be false. We therefore need to be cautious when we hear strange and magical things about Vedanta.

Let us now look at some esoteric misconceptions as well as at some simpler and more straightforward mistakes about Vedanta.

Vedanta is usually considered to be a uniquely Indian or, more specifically, a uniquely Hindu way of thinking. This is not correct. Let us illustrate by looking at some kind of parallel. By the middle of the twentieth century, the teaching of business administration had already brought popularity and good name to a number of excellent U.S.

schools. Thereafter, any discussion with a college student in India, planning to go abroad for a postgraduate degree in business administration, was never about which country to go to, but only about which school in the U.S. to go to! Thus, business administration seemed to have become a strictly American body of knowledge. However, we all know that businesses existed and were successfully administered in all parts of the world—this was so before the Old World even discovered America! So, it was not that business administration was purely American; it was only that America had developed and maintained a very successful and effective method of *teaching* business administration.

Similarly, the essence of Vedanta has been available to all humankind over all times and continents. Given the nature of Vedanta, it is true that relatively few people have been able to experience its full grandeur and that many of them have been in India; however, there have been throughout history people from a variety of different traditions, including Christianity, Islam, and Taoism, who have had the same kinds of experiences as those recorded in the Upanishads, and that too expressed in surprisingly similar language. So Vedanta is by no means only Indian or Hindu. It is the legacy of humankind as a whole, much as the pyramids (even though they happen to be in Egypt) or the law of gravity (even though it may have been first understood by an Englishman). What is uniquely Indian and Hindu is the tradition of *teaching* that body of knowledge which has been fully developed, preserved, and used in India over centuries. Because the Hindu religion is more a way of life than a system of sporadic rituals and because Vedanta needs a certain way of life before it can take root, the two became interrelated—the Hindu religion prepared individuals for Vedanta. But it is entirely possible to be receptive to Vedantic knowledge without any practice of the Vedic religion.

In like manner, it is not absolutely essential to be exposed to Vedantic knowledge only in the words of the Upanishads. In a broad sense, whichever language, whichever tradition, and whichever methodology brings to us knowledge of the true nature of our own self can be considered Vedanta. By the same token, if the objective of any process of teaching is not true and full self-knowledge, then it is not Vedanta in its spirit even if that process uses the Sanskrit language and the words of the Upanishads.

Another prevalent notion about Vedanta is that if it is valid and effective, then it must work like a quick fix! If it does not make instant sense or if it does not immediately start resolving our problems (physical, emotional, intellectual, and, perhaps, even financial!) than it is obviously worthless, so this thinking goes. Let us be clear that Vedanta is not a type of spell which will work mysteriously and instantly. So if we expect that some great change will occur when a fellow in orange robes and a flowing beard whispers a mantra in our ear, then we are in for a big disappointment. Similarly, please let us not believe that the touch, the gaze, or the mere silent presence of someone is necessarily going to work wonders for us. Nor should we believe that if we read the *Bhagavad Gita* once or listen to a discourse on an Upanishad, that in itself will trigger some remarkable change. Any knowledge requires some preparedness as a prerequisite, followed by investment of time and effort. It also requires some specific aptitude. In Vedanta we are dealing with the highest level of thought and intuitive vision known to humankind; we are dealing not with knowledge of one object or of one branch of information but with the very basis of all knowing. How can we hope to know enough about Vedanta to even have an opinion about it without a lot of time and effort having been spent under the guidance of an appropriate teacher? Many of us are not willing to put in the initial work to prepare ourselves to be fit enough even to be exposed to this teaching. It is therefore childish to expect this body of knowledge to reveal its true meaning and begin working for us on the basis of idle curiosity and desultory inquiry.

Further, while some parts of Vedanta will come to light more readily and bring results to sincere seekers even if they are not fully prepared, it needs to be made clear that the *full* depth of Vedanta is not open to everyone. This should not come as a surprise, because this is true of many other things. For some people the subject of advanced mathematics is and will remain a closed book; some others cannot distinguish between individual notes on a musical scale, no matter how much they try; some others seem completely unmoved by the beauty of language and literature. This is not to say that Vedanta is entirely the preserve of some special few. It is universal, it is fundamental, and it has something of great value for all seekers at all levels. We should, therefore, study it even as we recognize that its full vision may not be readily available to us.

We must also recognize at the outset that in whichever fashion Vedanta works for us, it is not going to have any *direct* impact on our surroundings and external problems. So, even after studying Vedanta, a person is likely to remain short of money and with asthma and with a quick temper if that is the way they were when they commenced their study. Vedanta is not intended to put financial planners and doctors out of business! This does not mean, on the other hand, that it makes no difference to anyone's life. While Vedanta has no direct effect on external problems, it has a great direct effect on our own mental state and radically changes our perceptions and our reactions in whichever situation we happen to be in. This improves our ability to face problems without getting too ruffled; it also enhances our competence to resolve many of those problems by lessening the fear, tension, and lack of objectivity which usually cloud our judgments and actions.

Another common impression that causes confusion is that Vedanta is a methodology for annihilating the mind, suppressing emotions, and erasing the ego. Nothing could be further from the truth. The mind is the mechanism by which we receive and interpret both external inputs (sense perceptions) and internal inputs (thoughts and memory); the same mind provides the color of emotions to these inputs in terms of *beautiful, pleasant, desirable, fearful, ugly* and so on; the intellect which provides discrimination and determines action is another facet of the mind; lastly, the ego, in terms of the *I*-sense (*I* enjoyed this, *I* did this, *I* know this . . .), is also part of the mind. We are in one way really nothing but the mind. As the mind is the resource used for knowing and doing anything and everything, the notion of using the mind to annihilate the mind does not make sense—unless one expects the mind to gracefully commit suicide! If the whole objective is to put the mind to sleep, then we do not need any knowledge other than the address of an obliging anesthetist or of a skillful barman. It is also quite pointless to work for a life without any emotions (which would make life utterly colorless) or to think of life without an ego (if we had no sense of *I*-ness and somebody called out our name, who would answer?).

Vedanta does not want us to learn some complex method of killing our mind. All that it tries to do is to make us see that the mind with all its facets is not us but a wonderful resource available to us and that we are much more than the mind. However, as all knowledge needs the mind, Vedanta has to work via our mind for this understanding too. It is in this context that Vedanta suggests that, as a preliminary step, we develop a better understanding of our mind so that the intellect can have a little more say instead of having powerful and binding emotions always ruling the roost. If we wanted to see our face in a pool of water it would not be sensible to empty out the pool, but it would be helpful not to keep dropping pebbles into that pool and thus creating continuous ripples! Any suggestions that Vedanta has in terms of control over the mind are really directed towards building a capability whereby emotions are a privilege to be enjoyed and not chains that bind us against our own wishes and against the call of our own intelligence.

However, emotions and likes and dislikes cannot just be wished away or willed away. An injunction to someone who is angry or sad to not be angry or sad is useless and potentially damaging; to whatever may be that person's existing problem, a further complex of guilt or worthlessness may be added by such an injunction: the person may feel that they were weak-minded to lose their temper in the first place and that they are now scaling new heights of weakness because they cannot control their anger even when a well-meaning friend (or teacher or book) sensibly asks them to do so. This sort of thing obviously does not get us far, and therefore Vedanta does not emphasize injunctions of "Do this" and "Do not do this." After all, if we could help it, who would choose to be uncontrollably angry or to be sad? What Vedanta does instead is encourage us to understand our mind better and teach us to effectively process our unwanted emotions instead of ignoring them or suppressing them. Learning to appropriately process emotions is, in fact, a very important part of the preparatory teachings of Vedanta.

Yet another notion about Vedanta which keeps some people away from it is that Vedanta involves or leads to asceticism and renunciation (a literal translation of the Sanskrit word *sannyasa*). Many think it to be a selfish and introverted pursuit which excludes the interest of family and friends. Others condemn it as being a cowardly retreat from the field of life into the safe but sterile realm of abstract intellectualization. Yet others believe it to be the source of an abject, fatalistic attitude and then try to establish some connection between this fatalism and India's social and economic problems.

We cannot overcome all this criticism by merely stating that it is ill-founded. The fact is that while each one of these views is incorrect, there are good reasons for such views to have arisen and to have remained prevalent. First of all, such views arise not in respect of the true and complete scheme of Vedanta but to limited segments taken out of context and so misused that the original intention is lost. Further, there are numerous types of followers and propounders of what passes as Vedantic knowledge. Many of these people are well-intentioned but have either not fully understood Vedanta themselves or are just not capable of conveying its message because they lack the personal qualities and training needed for teaching this somewhat abstruse subject. Others are people who, having gotten a smattering of Vedanta (at times just a collection of a few Sanskrit words and phrases), then go on to use that to trick other people whose good sense has taken a backseat due to pain or blind faith. Last comes the category of people who do not use Vedanta as a means of knowledge at all but as a means of comfort and hope to be clung to—and also to be preached with missionary fervor. All this leads to distortions and wrong conclusions, which then unfortunately are taken as real aspects of Vedanta. Let us now look at some of the criticisms which were mentioned earlier and see how they do not apply to Vedanta in its true sense.

Does Vedanta preach asceticism and renunciation? This conclusion seems to be justified based on some Upanishadic statements[5] as well as by some writings of great teachers

---

5. For instance the often recited verse from the *Mahanarayana Upanishad* which begins *na karmana, na prajaya, dhanena, tyagena eke amrit tatvam anshuhu*, meaning "Not by actions, not by having children, not by wealth, but only by renunciation is the immortal end achieved."

(Shankara's famous *Bhaja Govindam*[6]) and poets (Bhartruhari's *Vairagya Shatakam*[7]) which passionately and eloquently extol the virtues of renunciation. In this book we cannot get into an examination of the detailed meaning and context of such works. Let me just say that the objective of compositions like these is not to encourage everyone to don a loincloth, pick up a begging bowl, and wander off alone into the sunset! Some of this writing is exaggerated poetry due to an author having an upsurge of thought on a particular aspect at a given point in time; some of it is designed to shock people out of a complacent way of thinking. To get better measure of the real message of such writing, one needs to read a lot more of these authors. One also needs the help of a teacher to see the whole context and to understand that what is being talked about is not renunciation as a physical act but an attitude where what is really important is a fair and objective valuation of our concerns, possessions, and goals.

And our valuations do change with maturity and learning—a father who used to get very upset about misplacing his toys in his own childhood may now look upon his child throwing a tantrum about some lost marbles with benign indifference and gentle amusement. The child may find this attitude (of renunciation towards marbles) both infuriating and inexplicable. We all develop an attitude of renunciation to some previously dear objects as a result of time and our growth.

But what about people who don orange robes and

---

6. As an example, a translation of verse 18 reads: "Who can disturb a man's happiness if he can be happy living in the open halls of temples or under the trees, lying on the bare ground wrapped in skins, having given up every possession and enjoyment?"

7. Look at a translation of verse 31, again as an example: "In enjoyment, there is fear of disease; in social position, the fear of being displaced; in wealth, the fear of hostile kings; in honor, the fear of humiliation; in power, the fear of foes; in beauty, the fear of old age; in scriptural learning, the fear of opposing views; in virtue, the fear of seducers; in body, the fear of death. All things of this world connected with man are subject to fear; renunciation alone is fearlessness."

become wandering mendicants? Is this not a different and final kind of renunciation? Assuming that they have done this for a truly Vedantic pursuit (after mature thought and not as a reaction to failure in other fields), one has to recognize that a small number of people in all cultures and over all times have a mental make-up which encourages them to seek opportunities for intensive contemplation in solitude without distractions from any other agenda for themselves and for others around them. Such people may become monks, *bhikshus,* or *sannyasins* either on their own or within the ambit of some religious order. This does not mean that all people who wish to learn and benefit from Vedanta have to opt out of the normal mode of living. In fact the *Bhagavad Gita* goes to considerable length in pointing out that for a majority of people the path of carrying on with normal activities *(pravritti)* with the right understanding is far better than becoming a renunciate *(nivritti).*

Is Vedanta a selfish and self-centered pursuit? Should we even be asking this question in our times, when our most advanced societies pride themselves on permitting full freedom to each individual?! But let me try to answer this criticism more squarely. To the extent that Vedanta does involve gaining total and objective knowledge about our own self, it would appear somewhat self-centered and selfish. But this is only at an initial stage. Later, as more of the lessons of Vedanta are learnt and assimilated, the students' own jagged edges are dealt with; people pursuing Vedanta properly, in fact, become more comfortable and helpful persons to have around, with their empathy and lack of a driving personal agenda. In a way, the consequences of the proper pursuit of Vedanta can be compared (though obviously not as a full parallel) with the consequences of Adam Smith's vision of economic pursuit, whereby each individual, in attempting to maximize their own good, brings about the maximum good of society as a whole.

This discussion about Vedanta being selfish and self-centered reminds me of the story I was told of a king in an ancient kingdom (and Vedanta teachers use a large collection of stories to convey some views, at least at the initial stage). In his kingdom the tradition was for everyone to go around barefooted. One fine day when this king was out of his palace for a walk, his bare foot was pricked by a thorn. Very unreasonably he flew into a rage (kings will be kings!) and ordered his chief minister to ensure that the entire kingdom be covered in leather within one month, on pain of death. As the month passed and no visible action was being taken to carpet the entire kingdom with leather, the minister's enemies gleefully began to anticipate the poor man's end. On the appointed day the king summoned the minister and, with him in tow, went out of the palace to see if his instructions had been carried out. Obviously nothing at all had been done, and the king asked the minister if he had any explanations to give prior to being put to death. At this point the minister opened a package which he had been carrying and bent down towards the king's feet. When he rose, the king's feet had been clad in spanking new and beautiful leather shoes and the minister said, "Henceforth, sire, wherever you walk in your kingdom, it will be covered in leather for you!" Sometimes instead of looking at grand and impractical solutions in an attempt to solve everyone else's problems, it is more sensible to solve the problem at the individual level.

Even if the individual with whom the solution starts happens to be ourselves, this need not be considered particularly selfish. Our example may encourage others, and our ability to do our duty and help others will be greatly enhanced if we are not being continuously pricked by thorns ourselves. In a small and different way this is the basis when we are told in safety briefings on airplane flights that in the event of sudden cabin depressurization, we should don our own oxygen masks first, before helping children and others.

Further, if we really want to be less selfish then we owe people (and especially those whose welfare is our special concern) an opportunity to find expression of their full potential even if their way of doing so may not tally with what we ourselves want. In fact we owe them not only tolerance but, perhaps, even active encouragement. In Vedanta's view, an individual can fully grow only by pursuing self-knowledge; therefore, the ultimate value of any pursuit or relationship is to be reckoned by this measure.

In this context, let me mention Vedanta's vision of the purpose of marriage, as an instance of the importance placed on self-knowledge. The marriage ritual was to mark the beginning of a partnership wherein husband and wife set up home, made a living, raised children, participated in social and religious events, and generally led a full life in the ambit of righteousness. The initial objective was to fulfill normal physical, emotional, and social desires while contributing to the society in which one lived. But this was by no means the main purpose of marriage. Married life was to prepare both husband and wife for the ultimate pursuit of self-knowledge, which was to be undertaken at an appropriate stage when life on its usual plane had been fully lived and when a wealth of real-life experiences had been accumulated and were now available for mature analysis and reflection. If husband and wife could not collaborate and help each other in this culminating part of the journey of life then the marriage would not have fulfilled one of its most significant objectives. In this vision, marriage was really a holy alliance for humankind's highest purpose.[8]

---

8. In a more modern context it is worthwhile to note that the contemporary psychiatrist M. Scott Peck in his bestselling book *The Road Less Traveled* has defined love as "the will to extend one's self for the purpose of nurturing one's own or another's spiritual growth." This definition has several implications which go well beyond the usual notions of romantic love culminating in marriage (an institution which is then unfortunately and restrictively considered by many to be a vehicle for just having a good time in the comfort of mutual dependence).

Let us now turn to the fear that finding out more about Vedanta goes hand in hand with a retreat from "real life." This is truly ironical, because one of the major things that Vedanta helps us to understand, face up to, and live *is* real life. In fact Vedanta points out and proves that a shockingly large number of problems arise for human beings precisely because they ignore life's realities; it then invites us to use our discrimination and intelligence to understand what is real and what is a superimposition on the real and what are the different levels of "reality" that we encounter in day-to-day living. This is a very important part of Vedantic teachings. Vedanta actually brings a person closer to reality than anything else!

Further, if the word *retreat* used here carries with it connotations of cowardice then we should pause to consider what the full-fledged Vedantic pursuit may involve for the serious seeker: the giving up of a comfortable structure of notions and attitudes; deliberately turning away from commonly accepted goals and value systems; struggling with wisp-like thoughts and nuances couched in an unfamiliar idiom; risking commitment and effort to a hazy goal, which therefore means taking a plunge only on the strength of personal intuition and half-formed conviction; risking the wrath of and alienation from people who are near and dear. Truly, a person will not be able to last the full course of Vedanta unless they have an exceptional amount of strength and courage. (Here let me hasten to add that great strength and courage are needed when Vedanta becomes our sole pursuit; most of us are likely to study Vedanta as only one of our pursuits, and while this would still bring significant benefits, it would call for less than a dramatic level of bravery and risk-taking!)

What about the charge that Vedanta breeds a fatalistic attitude? Fatalism is an attitude caused by the acceptance of the doctrine that all events are predetermined for all times in such a manner that human beings are powerless to change them. Vedanta is supposed to preach such a doctrine (via the so-called theory of karma). This is a false and unfair conclusion. First of all the karma theory is not even part of the core teachings of Vedanta, as we shall see in the next chapter of this book. Further, for those who accept the karma theory, nowhere does it suggest even by implication that sitting back and letting events overcome us is the correct or the inevitable course to follow. In fact the teachings exhort us to awaken, to arise, and to actively deal with life and learning with vigor, skill, and intelligence. Lastly, as the *Bhagavad Gita* points out, given the nature of human beings, it is impossible for us to be truly actionless even for a moment; not only do involuntary physical actions (such as breathing) continue, but the mind also keeps on working and, more important, the very decision to remain apparently actionless is based on choice and acting upon that choice. We can of course ascribe our laziness to Vedanta, but that is not justified by its actual contents.

Also, at times, the genuine indifference of a person to some goals which were once important (and Vedanta does change the value usually placed on some of our goals) is taken as a mark of fatalism. There is a little story from Taoism about a frail, old Chinese master of Tao being accosted by a bunch of young and aggressive rowdies who tauntingly challenged the old man to a fight. They were quite startled when the master peacefully and quietly told them that it would be quite useless for them to fight him because he could never be defeated. Impressed by his lack of fear, they asked what made him feel so invincible. The old master answered that only those who wanted to win could be defeated—as he did not want to win this fight, there was no way in which they could defeat him! The point of this story is not to conclude that Vedanta (or Taoism) encourages us to be helplessly beaten up by any

passing bunch of toughs. The point sought to be emphasized is that it is possible to be indifferent to the result of
an activity if that whole activity holds no particular value
or importance to us. This indifference, based on discrimination, is obviously very different from fatalism.

Let us look at a few more notions about Vedanta. One
of the more popular one-liners quoted from Shankara's
writings is *brahma satyam jagat mithya,* translated as "The
ultimate reality is the only truth, and the world is illusory."
Leaving aside the bit about the ultimate reality, the second
part of that sentence (about the world being illusory) has
caused misconceptions and provoked humor. The misconception is that Vedanta tries to solve all human problems by
the simple trick of dismissing the whole world as unreal.
The humor is supposed to be reflected in questions (accom-
panied by appropriate sniggers) such as "So if the world is
an illusion, how come my toe hurts when I stub it against
this illusory table?" I will only point out at this stage that
the real meaning of the word *mithya* is neither *unreal* nor
illusory and that it is not the intention of Vedanta to prove
that the world is unreal. Vedanta says that the world is as
real as we are and has to be dealt with accordingly—
Vedanta is not a method which will help us to opt out of
living in and dealing with the world.

Part of the problem in using Vedantic concepts arises
when people apply them to only half of a situation. Here's
a story that illustrates this point: The great Shankara was
walking down a forest path with a group of his students,
when a maddened elephant suddenly emerged and charged
the group. The person who ran the fastest was Shankara
himself, who quickly climbed to the safety of a tall tree.
After the elephant went on its way, the perplexed students asked, "Master, you have taught that the world is
mithya. Why did you then run away from the mithya
elephant?" Shankara answered by asking, "How is that you

can see the charging elephant as mithya but cannot see my running also as mithya?" Whether historically accurate or not, the real point of this story is that it is not logical to apply a concept to only one half of a situation when the other half of that situation belongs to the same level of reality.

Another important wrong notion about Vedanta is that it is some sort of a religion. Religions are based on unverifiable beliefs (e.g.: there is an almighty being called God sitting in heaven; there is a hell for sinners; and so on). Religions appeal to faith and are not dependent on knowledge. They contain dogmas and use prescriptions. Vedanta is none of these things because it is knowledge-based and intended to give us a personal and direct experience of its teachings. It contains no dogmas and it does not even require us to believe in a heaven-bound Almighty Being keeping track of us and the entire creation. If at all it seems to contain prescriptions, they are really only descriptions of what many people have found useful in their own journeys towards a personal truth. If at all it has an overlay of Hindu religion it is only because of a congruency between the way of life prescribed under the Vedic religion and a preparatory way of life often found useful for the pursuit of Vedanta. In a strict sense one need not be a follower of Hinduism or any other religion, nor is there any strict necessity for belief in any particular God, to learn the lessons of Vedanta. (I must add, though, that most people would find it impossible to make the entire Vedantic journey without some recourse to an individually acceptable format of God. God here could be very different from the remote and inexplicable Supreme Being which religions usually postulate.)

Let me deal with one last type of misconception about Vedanta before we move on to the next chapter. This misconception revolves around some notion of equality.

This equality which Vedanta is supposed to promote takes many forms. So in one version, a person on the path of Vedanta is supposed to develop complete equality in their dealings with all beings in this world. In another version all persons who have reached the end of the Vedantic journey would have bodies with several identical characteristics (such as being impervious to physical suffering) and identical minds (no sadness, no preferences, no anger). In yet another view, the perfect world which Vedanta is apparently striving to create would have only "good" people living in peace and harmony, with no evil or unhappiness around. These are just some naive notions.

Neither Vedanta nor anything else is likely to make a normal human being want to cuddle a poisonous snake so as to put it on an equal footing with an adorable puppy. This is not what is meant by equality towards all. Equality here just means accepting that all creatures have their place in the scheme of the world and understanding them for what they objectively are. After this understanding, we continue to have the freedom to deal with any situation appropriately at the practical level. And at the practical level we have to behave differently depending upon the situation. For instance, once we understand and believe that all human beings deserve a certain level of respect and consideration because they are human beings, it does not have to be proved by bringing out our best dinnerware for a young children's party!

Also, it is not the intention of Vedanta to mass-produce enlightened clones. All persons who have received and fully understood the knowledge of Vedanta need not look and behave like the Buddha—in the Vedantic scheme of things there is scope for the body and mind to feel and react to physical and emotional pain, for the mind to have preferences, and for occasional flashes of temper even at the end of the journey. There is of course a tremendous difference between a person who has completed this journey and a person who has not, but enlightenment does not necessarily mean perfection in the conventional sense.

Coming to the notion of a world which is only good, let us clearly understand that the world as we know it exists only in polarity—all our states and even all our thoughts occur only because of their opposites. There is death only because of birth, a notion of beauty only because of a simultaneous notion of ugliness. We cannot have a world which is purely good, because we cannot even conceive of good unless evil is present. To attempt to have a world with its polarities removed is like trying to have a single-sided coin or wanting to see a movie on a screen where only white light is projected. There can of course be periods in history or some individual lives where the quality of goodness dominates. However, on a larger scale of time and space there has to be a balance not only between good and evil but also between all other polarities. Any hope of retaining only the good (or one end of any polarity) will never work, by the very nature of the world. That is why despite numerous good people, saints, and God's messengers (and, in some traditions, apparently God himself) having done their work on this Earth, evil continues quite unabated. Vedanta recognizes that creation has to be based on dualities and teaches people to understand and deal with them. While it encourages goodness, its primary aim is not to try to fulfill the impractical notion of a perfect world.

Chapter Three

◆

The Teachings

The Limitations of a Book

Before we get into the actual teachings of Vedanta, I would like to try to explain why reading a book is not the appropriate way of learning this subject and why there is no substitute for a proper teacher. This is not peculiar to Vedanta: there are many other situations in life where we cannot get away from direct learning with a real teacher. Let me start with a personal illustration. At a somewhat late stage in life I started learning to fly a small airplane and had exceptional difficulty in trying to land this craft. In this context a friend suggested that I practice with a well-known flight simulation program on a home computer. In a state of frustration I was willing to try anything, and so I went ahead and got this program and tried to use it to practice landings. To my horror, I discovered that flight simulation programs which run on home PCs not only failed miserably in simulating the experience of actually landing a light aircraft visually but, in fact, interfered with whatever tentative real-life landing skills I had already learnt! So, as far as I was concerned, there was no substitute for continuing to learn and practice in a real airplane with a real instructor. (Incidentally, for large commercial aircraft the training process does use multimillion-dollar simulators which are so real for all flight situations—including landings—that a pilot is fully qualified to fly a particular type of airplane without actually having set foot in a real version of that aircraft. However, no such substitute exists as yet for small aircraft—nor does one seem likely for teachers of Vedanta!)

In this illustration we only looked at a situation where a particular type of skill could not be learnt by an indirect method. Now let us look at something which does not involve any physical skill or dexterity, but just knowledge.

We all know that words have to be used for the purpose of conveying knowledge. However, there are instances where words do not convey any knowledge. This may come as a surprise, because we mostly take the literal and direct meaning of words, as they are, to obtain the knowledge that we seek. And usually we are justified in doing this. So, if a person asks, "What is the distance between Bombay and London?" and someone replies "Five thousand miles," the questioner would be correct in looking at the literal meaning of the words *five thousand miles* for directly obtaining the knowledge that they want. Now, if the same person wanted to know something about Einstein's theory of relativity and a book tried to give them some of its basic concepts by using words like "Time and space are inter-changeable,"[9] where would that leave them? The words could be very accurate and the person would understand the meaning of each word—they would know what *time* is, what *space* is, and what *interchangeable* means. Does the sentence however convey the knowledge it is intended to? Would the person now know anything about relativity that

---

9. This is a loose version of the more accurate phrase "Time-Space Continuum." I have deliberately taken this liberty to emphasize the point that common words need to be looked at in uncommon ways in special situations.

they could really comprehend and assimilate? Is the statement "Time and space are interchangeable" the same kind of knowledge as the statement "Fire is hot"? Unless the questioner has a background in modern physics, these words would convey no real knowledge to the person even though they appear to do so.

Statements like "Time and space are interchangeable" do not convey their full meaning even when they are amplified with more words. Each explanation just leads to further questions. There is a twofold reason for this. First, studying the theory of relativity assumes that the student has a sufficient background in classical physics and mathematics. Second, subjects like relativity (or quantum mechanics or astrophysics) are at the very edge and beyond the envelope of our conventional knowledge. To deal with this kind of fundamentally different knowledge requires an almost intuitive ability to think and make a whole paradigm shift. Many of us are just not capable of doing this. It is for this reason that even qualified physicists may not be able to always fully understand the theories of scientists of a different breed like Max Planck, Albert Einstein, and Stephen Hawking. Real understanding of such knowledge needs both the inputs of a master of the subject and an appropriately prepared and endowed student. Similarly, there are portions of Vedanta which go beyond usual thought and beyond the bounds of our usual logic. Here too we can only use words to deal with these matters, but we have to look for radically different meanings and unfamiliar sense coming out of familiar words.

One can, of course, choose not to get into these sublime reaches of Vedanta because great effort and aptitude are required. This is no reason to drop Vedanta completely; there is a lot to learn and benefit from even in Vedanta's more accessible teachings. In science too we can ignore relativity, quantum mechanics, and astrophysics and yet use other bits of science and technology to improve our lives. (In fact, on a day-to-day basis, we do not even need the knowledge that the sun is actually stationary while it appears to rise, travel, and set every day.) However, some of us are more keen to expand our horizons and have both the ability and the willingness to grapple with the fuzziness at the boundaries of conventional knowledge and to leap-frog over some apparently logical steps to go beyond these boundaries.

So, as we look at the teachings of Vedanta we need to assess our own abilities and interest to decide how far we want to go and in which direction. In this process it is quite sensible to first use those portions of Vedanta which make sense more readily. In fact, a majority of people in their spiritual quest never go beyond *bhakti* (worship of a personal God) or *karma yoga* (carrying on with the usual activities of a normal, ethical life with a certain special attitude towards results). The teachers of such aspects of spirituality (who often blend some portions of Vedanta with religion) have mass followings. Followers derive comfort, purpose, and satisfaction from these teachings. In turn, society as a whole benefits. However, as far as Vedanta is concerned, such teachings are only preparatory or peripheral in nature.

The totality of Vedanta goes much further into several different levels of meaning and complexity. The deeper one goes, the more rigorous are the demands on the intellect, the emotions, and the intuitive powers of the student. There is nothing wrong with someone stopping at a level where they are comfortable and can cope. What is wrong is to come to a sweeping conclusion that what may not be relevant to us becomes irrelevant *per se* or, even more inexcusably, that what cannot be understood by us has to be useless or illogical.

This reminds me of something which my father used to do. He was a man with many excellent qualities—but the ability to appreciate classical Hindustani music was not one of them! I used to like and often listened to a very famous male vocalist of this tradition. A common practice in this style of singing is for the singer to occasionally extend one arm fully and bend the other arm at the elbow so that its palm touches one of the singer's own ears; this happens more so when long and high notes are being hit by his voice. I would be engrossed in listening to and watching this artist on television when my father would triumphantly interrupt by saying "I am not the only one who thinks this singing is terrible. He himself thinks so! See how he is shutting off his own ears!" This is not to suggest that everyone should like all types of music. However, we are not justified in concluding that music which we personally do not like is not music at all. Further, in not liking a particular style of music, we are denied one more avenue of enjoyment. When our prejudice, inability, or indifference is with reference to some really fundamental knowledge, it may not affect us within the sphere in which we usually operate but, whether we know it or not, we are denying ourselves an opportunity to expand our boundaries.

Let us look at one last category of situations where no amount of information or words would actually convey the true nature of what is sought to be conveyed. A good example would be an emotion like deep love between a man and a woman. Do you think that by reading Shakespeare's beautiful love sonnets or by reading learned books on this emotion, anyone can ever get the actual taste and feel of love? We can never fully know love except by being in love ourselves. There is no substitute for direct, personal experience in this type of knowing. It is something like trying to see a 3-D image from a stereograph. We can stare at the meaningless jumble of dots, we can listen to helpful instructions to relax and let our eyes focus at a point beyond the picture, and so on. The actual picture hidden in the mass of dots can be described to us in detail. But all this really leads nowhere till we suddenly see a vibrant and clear picture with depth and color emerge from the apparently stray patterns of dots. We see when we see!

Obtaining full vision of the teachings of Vedanta requires skills and practice; it requires specific preparation and special aptitude; it needs a change in orientation in the way in which we see and understand things; it needs a different kind of wisdom. In our present age of reliance on quantitative methods and instantaneous transfer of masses of accurate data we tend to confuse information with wisdom. Information can be conveyed by words, numbers, and symbols. This cannot be done for wisdom. Knowledge at and beyond the edge of our current understanding needs a different kind of knowing. In such situations usual logic and structured process, though still useful, begin to run up against their own inherent limitations. This is why we need an expert teacher, and why we ourselves need to meet some rigorous preconditions.

I should also point out here that there are even more fundamental reasons why some of Vedanta's teachings cannot be understood and corroborated in the usual manner. This has to do with the fact that Vedanta is an independent means of knowledge and its topic is the *I* who is behind all experiencing and knowing. We will deal with these aspects later in this chapter and in subsequent chapters, as we go along. However, it is important to remember that ultimately Vedanta is not a subject to be only studied but a path to be personally walked; a shortcut or a second-hand approach does not work here beyond a point.

With all these explanations, caveats, and disclaimers, let me finally proceed with spelling out some Vedantic teachings. While Vedanta itself has no particular classification of its teachings, for the purpose of this chapter I am going to deal with the matter under three broad headings: *Preparatory Teachings, Core Teachings,* and *Peripheral Teachings.* These divisions are subjective and merely for convenience. They should not be looked upon as some rigid and sequential classification.

Preparatory Teachings

We have already seen that to study any subject requires a certain amount of advance preparation. The usual preparation required for Vedanta includes the achievement of a degree of thinking ability, emotional stability, and maturity. A level of morality and humanity is essential. A collection of experiences drawn from life itself is also needed. (There are many other qualities and preconditions required of a serious student of Vedanta, but here we will restrict ourselves only to some basic ones for gaining a quick appreciation of what the preparation involves.) How are these qualities and conditions to be achieved? In the India of Vedic times these were sought to be brought about by a way of life enjoined by religion and convention which directly and indirectly prepared people for the goal of the pursuit of Vedanta. While for most of us today this ancient structure of society has no direct or practical relevance, it is still useful to look at it to admire not only its wisdom and utility but also its underlying understanding of basic human nature and needs which have not changed with time.

In Vedic times the life of a Hindu was seen as divided into four stages, and each stage had its own structure and goals. These stages were *brahmacharya* (being a student), *grihastha* (being a householder), *vanaprastha* (being in the process of withdrawing from usual work and family duties—a sort of retirement), and *sannyasa* (totally dedicating oneself to the Vedantic pursuit with no other commitment whatsoever).

As a student, the scheme for an eligible young person was to live for several years with a teacher and his family amongst other students. Apart from studying, the student had to work on the upkeep and maintenance of the school *(ashram)* property and be of personal service to the teacher and his wife. This engendered a sense of humility, a spirit of accommodation, and an appreciation of the effort and dignity in physical labor. Various academic subjects were taught at the ashram, including grammar, poetry, and logic. This, amongst other uses, was to help in proper understanding and analysis of the Vedas and other texts. The Vedas were dealt with especially in terms of prayers and rituals; the Upanishadic portions were also covered, but more as a preliminary exposition because the students lacked the age and maturity to understand their true meaning. Religion and ethics were taught and practiced. The teaching also covered a variety of practical skills and knowledge such as science, mathematics, and economics. All this developed logical and intellectual abilities and provided a grounding for making a living in the world.

Ashrams were usually located in forests or on riverbanks amidst nature and away from towns and cities. The leading of a controlled and ethical life with the teacher and exposure to the discipline and norms of the Vedic religion at the ashram provided students with a full appreciation of a non-invasive way of living which kept them in harmony with nature, other beings, and their own selves. An exposure to the philosophy of the Upanishads planted some seeds in the minds of the students which would sprout much later when they would be ready for the stage of Vedantic pursuit.

After completing the well-rounded course of true education here, the student was ready for the next stage, of entering the world as a working and family person. (The *Taittiriya Upanishad* contains an example of a graduation speech made by a teacher to his students at the time of leaving the ashram. It contains beautifully simple and practical parting reminders on how to conduct worldly life.)

As an adult, this educated individual then married, made a living, raised a family, and participated in social and religious events. This was the stage when economic activity and pleasures were pursued. In the Vedic way of thinking, the four objectives of any human being *(purushartha)* are *artha* (economic, physical, and emotional security), *kama* (pleasures—physical, emotional, and aesthetic), *dharma* (righteousness), and *moksha* (liberation from universal and fundamental self-ignorance). As a householder, the person had full scope to pursue success and pleasures, but with the condition that these pursuits be within the ambit of righteousness as laid out by religious texts and interpreted by wise elders. This provided a channel for the fulfillment of normal human desires for security, recognition, and pleasure. It also recognized the fact that when driven by our desires, if we do not have the restraint of dharma, it does not take long to start trampling upon other people's rights and ignoring our own innate sense of right and wrong. When we go against universal values which we all instinctively and invariably know, we face a dichotomy within our own selves between what we know is right and what we are actually doing or thinking. Such an internal division takes place every time fundamental values are transgressed and this, in turn, prevents the mind from remaining collected and undisturbed. And this disturbance occurs even if the division of the mind is at the subconscious level.

We will not be able to examine such values and understand their importance here because that is a large topic by itself. We will just note that a significant part of the preparation for Vedanta was not only in working out normal human desires but also in ensuring that, in this process, the result was not a society robbed of tolerance and fellowship or minds robbed of peace and equanimity. Apart from considerations of ethics and social good, such a society and such minds would be great hindrances in any meaningful Vedantic pursuit. For this important reason householders were kept continually aware of dharma, which they had studied as students.

As far as an individual was concerned, the initial incentive to lead an ethical and religious life was not so much preparation for the ultimate pursuit of Vedanta but more a belief in continuous rebirths and the possibility of heaven. Right actions were expected to attract God's grace, which would not only make the current life more happy and comfortable but also lead to greater fortune when the individual soul was reborn in a new body after the death of the current body. With a very large accumulation of grace, the soul could be admitted to heaven, where the pains and afflictions of an earthly body did not exist and where pleasures abounded. As these were simply beliefs, there was no way of proving (or disproving) them; however, they had their value, as they promoted ethics and righteousness.

In spite of such beliefs there was always the possibility of greed and passion driving one away from the path of virtue. It was therefore necessary to be constantly watchful, never forgetting dharma and not permitting damaging emotions and tendencies to accumulate. This was encouraged, amongst other things, by periodic prayer and rituals. Some of these prayers and rituals were daily. They were in some ways like a daily shower. In the process of living we collect small amounts of dirt, perspiration, and the like on a daily basis. If we did not shower regularly, we might find that many people would not be willing to live near us! Similarly, in the process of living we also collect daily a bit of anger, greed, jealousy, hatred, and so on. These stick to the mind and accumulate. Unless we clean and discharge our mind frequently, these negative emotions and tendencies would build up to unmanageable proportions. Therefore one of the requirements of a life of dharma was a small ritual and prayer thrice a day (at dawn, noon, and dusk). The very act of prayer was designed to remind an individual of higher values, renew a sense of humility and gratitude for what they already had, and encourage them to see themselves not as a mere individual pitched against the world but as part of a greater reality.

Prayers and rituals were also required at important milestones such as births, marriages, shifting to a new house, the change of seasons, and deaths. Again the intention was to provide the individual an opportunity to let God into their life, be a little more humble, and permit better interconnection with the community (because many rituals required inviting everyone in the locality). This system also brought about some solemnity and significance to important events and provided a sense of belonging and a sense of worth to each individual.

Daily prayer *(nitya karma)* as well as prayer and ritual on specified special occasions *(naimittika karma)* were considered compulsory. There were other optional prayers and rituals for obtaining special favors from the creator (e.g., a child, the end of a drought, the curing of a disease). Some more were suggested for repentance of wrongs done. The rituals themselves were not meaningless, because each ritual had a very intelligent scientific, psychological, or economic rationale if one cared to go behind the overt action and words. However, what was even more important in all this was the attitude and the consequences it had of producing a peaceful mind with a sense of humility and freedom from too much fear, guilt, anger, and remorse. For instance, elaborate ceremonies after the death of a parent provided an avenue for the required consolation and healing. At a very pained and vulnerable time, one was surrounded by family, community, and priests. By doing rituals for the good of the dead person's soul, the individual dealt to some extent with their sense of loss, and perhaps guilt, for not having behaved appropriately during the dead person's lifetime. And this was quite irrespective of whether there was in fact a soul or not and whether or not such rituals had any real impact on any soul.

There was an attempt also to carry over this sane and healthy approach to other areas of day-to-day life outside prayers and rituals. In the process of making a living and dealing with the world, a person would be continuously acting, driven by desire or a sense of duty. All action is of course undertaken with the expectation of a particular result. So if we invest in stocks we expect a certain increment, when we attend a concert we expect to obtain some enjoyment, and when we perform an act of kindness we expect kindness in return, or at least a word or look of appreciation. This is perfectly natural. However, our experience is that actions rarely produce exactly the result anticipated. The actual result of any action is likely to be either more than or less than anticipated, with relatively few occasions when the result is exactly as envisaged before the action. If the result is more than expected, one is likely to be carried away by an upsurge of happiness and pride—it was *my* thinking, *my* doing, *my* patience, *my* determination which brought about this fantastic result! If the result is in line with expectation then that too is a cause of happiness and pride (perhaps a little more subdued) for the same reasons. However, if the result is less than or contrary to expectations then obviously there is scope for unhappiness as well as for remorse, guilt, blame, and enmity. It was recognized that these violent and uncontrolled swings of the mental pendulum from elation to despair had to be regulated. This was needed both to bring some abiding peace and balance in the daily life of an ordinary person and to prepare their mind for a deeper and more contemplative pursuit later.

There were two main attitudes towards actions and their results which were suggested to bring about such mental regulation. They were designed to be useful for two different kinds of mindsets commonly found amongst people. In India, these two approaches are well-known by the terms used for them in the *Bhagavad Gita*: *bhakti* and *karma*. *Bhakti* (meaning worship of and devotion to God) was an attitude encouraged for those who were quieter, less driven, and more pious. Such people were not sannyasins, but would consider devotion to their chosen form of a personal God (and there was a large choice available from the pantheon of deities) as the most important purpose of their lives. Once devotion and worship attained this prime status for such individuals, it automatically and simultaneously reduced the importance of other actions and removed undue concern about the results of actions undertaken to fulfill worldly needs and duties. A large part of their fulfillment and satisfaction came not from actions which bloated the ego but from devotion to God, where the ego did not have a larger-than-life role. This path of bhakti continues to be very important in India even today and has the benefit of a large number of spiritual and religious teachers as well as mass following. It has developed as a full-fledged philosophy by itself with several well-known traditions. However, as far as Vedanta is concerned, the path of devotion and worship, though important, is really in the nature of preparation for learning about the true nature of our own self.

But what about those who are not particularly enraptured by a life centered around a personal God? What about people who have the energy and desire for more tangible achievements? For such people the karma aspect of life was emphasized. *Karma* means "action," and some ground rules are needed on the path of action relevant to the doer and the achiever. How does such a person keep their mind from swinging between the extremes of great happiness and great unhappiness? To tell them not to act at all would be ridiculous, because no human being can remain actionless, much less this type of person, who has full measure of energy and desire to achieve visible progress. To tell such a person to act without expecting any result would be even more ridiculous. Why would anyone act if they did not expect a specific result, and how is it humanly possible to divorce action from its expected result? After all, if one gets into an airplane to go to a particular city, one certainly has an expectation of reaching one's destination; if one does a physical workout regularly, it is certainly with the expectation of being in better shape and health. The solution lies not in erasing expectations (which is the dangerously false interpretation of a famous verse[10] from the *Bhagavad Gita*) but in developing an intelligent approach to the actual results of any action. As we have seen, when the results of our actions are equal to or more than expectations then there is scope for elation, and when the results are less than or contrary to expectations then there is scope for despondency. We can have a more balanced reaction to results only if we can see that the input by way of our action is never the sole determinant of the actual result.

How do we see this? Again we can use two different approaches, depending upon our mental make-up. If we are comfortable with the concept of God as the creator, sustainer, and resolver of all creation including ourselves, then we could look upon results of our action as *prasada*. The word *prasada* cannot be really translated into a single English word. It has connotations of something returned by or given by God with his grace and blessings. When people go to a Hindu temple the priest will give to each person, as they are about to leave, a little something which has been offered to or which has touched the idol of God. This could be a few drops of water or milk (used for washing the idol) or a few leaves of *tulsi* (a plant considered holy and used in temples) or some sugar crystals or a morsel of cooked food (which has been offered to the idol) or even a pinch of some

10. *Karmanye va adhikaraste ma phaleshu kadachana:* "You have a right only to act but no rights over results of your action."—*Bhagavad Gita* 2:47

ash (from incense sticks lit before the idol). The beautiful thing about prasada is that one accepts it with joy and full satisfaction because it comes from God. Here it does not matter whether the prasada is in the form of water, leaves, food, or ashes, because the attitude of reverence and gratitude it generates does not depend on the actual form of the prasada. In daily living, some people are able to look upon the results of all their actions as prasada from God and are thus able to remain free of major mental upheavals irrespective of the nature of the actual results of their actions. This solves the problem for them.

Others however have difficulty in being able to look upon all results of their daily actions as prasada. People with such a mental orientation are encouraged to rationally analyze their own actions and consequent results and see for themselves how many things beyond their own control (and even beyond their imagination) enter into the making of a particular result. For instance, if we start a new business then our planning, our skills, our special knowledge, our capital, and our hard work certainly have a critical bearing on the success of the business. But are these the only factors? What about things like the fortuitous closing down of a competitor or the supportive confidence of a banker or a favorable change in taxation policies or the absence of natural disasters or the finding of an exceptionally talented and committed manager? If any of us do enough honest thinking about major results which have affected our lives (for good or for bad), we cannot but conclude that while any action is ours, the result of that action is a product of several people, events, and circumstances beyond our control and, often, beyond our knowledge. If this lesson is learnt well and one is frequently reminded of it by teachers, books, and one's own thinking then it certainly helps to reduce the amplitude of mental swings. Such lessons and reminders were made into an integral part of the life of the person in the *grihastha* stage of life. This approach to an action-oriented life became a vital way of preparation for the active person so that ultimately they would be ready for Vedanta.

It will have been noticed that the entire traditional scheme of life for a householder was geared to protect and build up a healthy ego without letting it assume unnaturally large proportions. It provided an opportunity for sublimating emotions by fulfilling them where appropriate or, otherwise, by providing social and psychological mechanisms to adequately process them so that they did not build up unhealthy pressures either in the conscious or subconscious mind. The whole setup not only made for a reasonably happy and contented life but also provided vital preparation for further stages of growth and evolution. The grihastha's last major duty was to get their children married. After grandchildren made their appearance it was time for transition to the next stage: vanaprastha.

Vanaprastha was a time of withdrawal as well as a time for deriving some lessons from the experiences of the full and busy life so far. By permitting their children, who were now grown up, to handle financial and social matters, they were giving their offspring an opportunity to learn and grow in the supportive presence of retiring parents and other elders. This also avoided the conflict between generations which arises when both want to do the same thing and at the same time but in different ways. But above all, this period was a time for the matured householder to draw some deeper meanings from life. With what vision and goals had one started life as a young person? How many goals had been fulfilled? How many still mattered? What were major successes and failures? Were all failures avoidable? Did all successes deliver their promise? How long did satisfaction, joy, and contentment from any success last? Was one comfortable with life, its meaning, and the prospect of death? As a result of such questioning and introspection, a mature and experienced person could come to the conclusion that even after living a full and satisfying life, there were many fundamental questions which remain unanswered and, perhaps, even unasked. If there had been major failures and voids in their life, then even more valuable lessons could be drawn.

Not all people in the vanaprastha stage came to the same conclusions out of their experiences, but for some of them the realization dawned that no amount of effort and achievements can ever bring complete and abiding fulfillment. To be successful by becoming something (rich, skilled, healthy, famous) required sacrifice and effort apart from good luck; to fail of course hurt; to protect the fruits of success required further effort; the possibility of loss of success was always a continuous fear; worst of all, success was like a receding horizon which moved with one, and one never quite got there. Any achievement only provided temporary respite from the thirst to become something other than whatever one was—even if one worked only to maintain a status quo, it was an effort to be *other than* an insecure individual, fearful of change in the present situation. To quench this thirst only by more achievements or by attempts to hang on to whatever one had already achieved was like trying to satisfy a fire by feeding it with fuel—the attempt was doomed even before it commenced! One was thus led to the conclusion that either the proposition that there could be lasting joy and contentment was false or that one had been looking for joy and contentment at the wrong place and in the wrong manner. Here, the words of the Upanishads, studied without full understanding in student days, came back to some of these contemplators and there was now an urge to revisit the wisdom contained therein, which promised to solve the fundamental human problem in a completely different way.

This is where, for a few people, the need to find final

answers to the meaning of life and its struggles became so great that nothing else mattered. They then gave up all possessions, connections, and other aspirations and concentrated solely on the study of the great truths of the Upanishads under the guidance of an expert teacher. This was the last stage of life—*sannyasa*—when there was no commitment to anybody or anything else except to find personal answers to fundamental questions. This is how life and the method of living prepared persons for the pursuit of Vedanta in the traditional way in India.

From all this it would be wrong to conclude that in ancient India all people ultimately became sannyasins or that Vedanta could be pursued only in ripe old age, and that too only after becoming a sannyasin. The four stages of life and what was to happen in each stage was only one model out of many possibilities. Many people discovered the relevance and joy of Vedanta much earlier, when they were in the grihastha stage. For a majority of people the vanaprastha stage did not bring about a disenchantment with the usual approach to happiness, and they proceeded to old age with views which were substantially unchanged since becoming adults. However, adherence to bhakti and karma with the appropriate attitudes and the general setup of society as a whole helped to maintain a level of balance and satisfaction. Even for those who did become disenchanted, sannyasa and the pursuit of Vedanta was not the only possibility. Some never took to Vedanta at all; yet others pursued Vedanta without ever having the need to become sannyasins.

But how is all this relevant to us in our age and time? Our type of education, social setup, and value system are totally different now. How do we deal with the preparation for the pursuit of Vedanta, which seems to require an alien and unworkable lifestyle? Even more fundamentally, do we need Vedanta at all today?

To answer the last question first, it seems to me that

Vedanta is more relevant to all of us today than perhaps in any other time. We live in highly charged times when people, events, and technology are whizzing past us, but in spite of our great speed and activity we are not quite sure about where we are actually going. Our faster pace of life may mask fundamental problems and questions temporarily, but these can never be resolved by what we usually consider progress. Progress in our present civilization seems to mean converting into a necessity what was once a privilege or a luxury. In my own lifetime I have been closely connected with people who started life with walking as the basic means of transport due to economic reasons; they then went on to acquire bicycles, which soon became essential; much later they acquired motorcars, and then if the car was in the garage for servicing for a day, it became a really annoying hardship. I also know people who feel deprived because their private jet is already a few years old and they have not yet got the latest replacement which is bigger, faster, and fancier! The point here is not to suggest that there is something particularly noble about walking as a means of transport or that it is sinful to want the latest version of an executive jet. But, on the other hand, if one wants to retain any sensible perspective about increasing levels of comfort and convenience, it is vital to clearly know that we very quickly get used to them, that our thermostats reset themselves at a higher level, and that new baselines are drawn whereby the amount of joy and satisfaction which can be derived from such things always sharply declines in a short time. It is therefore futile to expect lasting joy and satisfaction from such achievements. We, paradoxically enough, need to cope with the disappointment from our greater comforts themselves because they yet leave large parts of our inner recesses untouched and thirsting.

In this context it is useful to understand that technology,

in which we have so much faith and hope, traps us into new problems even as it releases us from old ones. Not too long ago even large Indian cities used the old, mechanical telephone exchange systems. The now antiquated telephone instruments all had cumbersome rotary dials. However, because the system was not so fast and reliable, one tended to make fewer and shorter calls and also accepted the fact that a person could be incommunicado, especially if that person traveled to small towns and villages. Now we have electronic exchanges with pushbutton phones. Communication is certainly easier and more reliable, but not without a price. The number of digits that we have to dial has increased dramatically—we end up dialing telephone card numbers as well as access codes, country codes, and city codes before we actually get to dialing a phone number. We might then get an answering system with a menu where we have to dial more digits to make a selection. Also, with electronic technology, we may not get a busy signal but, instead, can be put in a telephone queue where one cannot gauge how long it will be before actually speaking to a human being or even to a machine! Lastly, the very fact that we can make a telephone call from almost any location, including airplanes, reduces the amount of free and unpressured time which the old technology forced upon us. And this type of effect is true of many other areas.

As another instance, while technology has certainly improved our ability to provide better healthcare, it has also perhaps increased the concerns we have about health. With better testing and investigative techniques we are now aware of new diseases and are also concerned about detecting old diseases earlier. Further, drugs such as antibiotics, while they have helped to save countless lives, have also led to carelessness and to mutations in disease-causing organisms which then make them immune to our armory of drugs. As yet another example, more reliable aircraft technology has led to higher speeds, bigger airplanes, and more air travelers. Accidents and crashes are far fewer, but when they happen they are usually catastrophic and involve a very large number of people. Technology is not without its double edges.

All this is not to say that we should reject technology or refuse scientific progress. Progress in technology is fundamental in increasing our capabilities and improving our standards of living as a whole race. At the individual level also, all of us find it useful and even imperative to adopt and adapt to such current technology as is relevant to our particular lives. There are no basic contradictions between science and technology on the one hand and growth by self-knowledge on the other hand. In fact, for most people, an antagonistic attitude to the prevalent applications of science and technology is likely to impose needless constraints and create an atmosphere of futile opposition in their own environment. Such a state can hardly be conducive to inner growth and objective understanding. The point is that, as we participate in current progress, we should not have some unrealistic expectation that science and technology are only a win-win game or that they will ever solve some types of fundamental human problems.

One other thing which is glaring in our present social setup (and more so in successful and developed economies) is the relative insignificance of the individual human being. While the consumer is supposed to be king or queen and each individual is probably healthier, better nourished, better clothed, and better informed than ever before, there is no getting away from the fact that we feel more cut off and less significant as individuals. Families are smaller and either break up or disperse more readily; there is an immense difference between personal interaction and being in touch with family, friends, and, indeed, the whole world while hunched alone over a keyboard and staring at a computer screen in a closed room. Airports are gigantic;

hotel lobbies are huge; shopping malls sprawl over acres; movie theatres have dozens of screens; hospitals have a thousand beds; cityscapes are full of high-rise buildings; roads and bridges are choked with cars. All this very often leads to a feeling of being an immaterial part of a faceless herd or being merely a statistic which needs to be agglomerated with a million others to be considered useful only as part of a database. The sheer scale of our systems and structures makes us feel lost and dwarfed. We see this when we stand at a busy intersection in Manhattan and look up at towering buildings all around us; we also know that this feeling is completely different from being dwarfed by the Himalayas in India or by the redwood trees in California or even by the cathedral in Cologne. This again is not some nostalgic plea to hark back to the good old days. The sensible lesson to draw from the current way of life is to realize that we owe an even greater responsibility (to ourselves and to those whose lives we can affect) to consciously work out a personal philosophy which will provide a stable reference point amidst frenetic activity, to nurture the spirit in a feast which only caters to the senses and emotions, and to reestablish our connection with totality by objective understanding.

As was said earlier, this is rendered difficult by our educational, social, and economic systems and the virtual disappearance of meaningful religion or nurturing philosophy. However, this sword cuts with both its edges. Our successes are much more rapid, but we can experience our unquenched thirst for meaning and fulfillment more quickly and in the midst of apparent plenty. Our failures inflict much harsher punishment, because large portions of society have no time and place for those who have not made it. We can experience loneliness amidst the glittering lights and swirling crowds of people in our great cities; we can feel a deep sense of impoverishment even as we

surround ourselves with pension schemes and mutual fund
investments—things which should make us feel rich and
secure. We are well aware of rapid scientific progress and
are also aware how quickly each new finding displaces an
apparently solid old finding. All this does lead some of us
to look for deeper meaning outside the usual schemes of
finding happiness and contentment. I do believe that for
many of us our present style of life does, however uninten-
tionally, push us towards wisdom like Vedanta.

Today, if and when we turn to Vedanta, we may not possess some of the formal and well-thought-out preparatory
experiences which ancient Indian tradition made available.
We may have no knowledge at all of the Vedas; religion and
its tempering and healing effects may not be as readily
available for many of us; we may be conditioned to believe
that instantaneous and complete gratification of all our
desires and emotions is not only our birthright but also a
duty which the world owes us. If we are to profitably use
Vedanta and also get over our strong prejudices and conditioning today, then we really do need the good fortune of
finding a kind and competent teacher. We also need extra
skill to be able to see the relevance and validity of this
ancient wisdom in today's context. The truth, by definition,
can never change; Vedanta deals with some fundamental
truths and we need to use our well-developed intelligence
and experience to see those truths blaze before us with a
light no dimmer than what has radiated since the beginning
of time, even though our setting and social conditions are
different. When the *Bhagavad Gita* says *yogah karmasu
kaushalam (yoga is skill in action)* it does not mean that
skill in picking a pocket or in carrying out complex surgery
is going to lead us to the wisdom of the ages—it really
means that we need to be skillful in seeing and properly
applying the tenets of religion, ethics, and philosophy in
our daily lives as they are now and thus prepare ourselves

to be receptive to knowledge which will deal with the age-old fundamental human problem at its very root.

One of our problems now (at least for many of us) is that we think that occasional dalliance with dharma is a great and special achievement. We look upon artha (security) and kama (pleasure) as normal human aspirations, and look upon being concerned with dharma as an interesting oddity; moksha (liberation by self-knowledge) never even seriously crosses the boundary of our horizons. However, the fact is that there is nothing special about artha and kama—squirrels store nuts as security for winter, and all living things make efforts to be comfortable, to play, to rest, and to procreate. Only human beings can have the goal of dharma; to be conscious of righteousness and to select it as an important objective is not only a uniquely human privilege but is, in fact, a special human duty. A human being completely unconcerned with dharma misses out on something which makes humans different from other living beings; without having first imbued dharma with a status higher than artha and kama, it is very difficult to see the real value of moksha. The challenge in our day and time is to bring some more specially human concerns into our lives in spite of a general sense of apathy towards dharma. And what is needed, to begin with, is not some labored attempt at ethical perfection but a sincere attempt to understand the real value of trying to live by the values required by dharma.

While saintliness is needed to scale the ultimate heights of Vedantic teaching, a large part of the scope and beauty of Vedanta becomes available to us as soon as our attitude to dharma changes even a little, upon beginning to appreciate its true value. A great beginning is possible by just leaning towards righteousness; only a modicum of realism, humility, compassion, and gratitude is needed to reawaken our lost awe and wonder in life and living. This task is greatly helped if one can turn, from time to time, to a personal God. Communication with God is vital in any spiritual pursuit and more so at a preparatory stage.

The concept of God is charged with emotion and surrounded by opinions and notions. While it is beyond the scope of this book to enter into a detailed discussion on God, it has to be said that proper recognition and acceptance of God is an emotional and psychological necessity and a vital part of the preparatory work. Without an altar which one can approach with faith, love, and trust, a person can reach a dead end of mental and emotional negativity and confusion where no other human being can be of much help. Only God can help here, not by waving a magic wand and changing our external circumstances, but by providing a means of discharging negativity from both our conscious and subconscious mind and by promoting positive and healing emotions, again coming from our own mind. While many find comfort in a form of God coming from whichever religious tradition they belong to, we are at liberty to create a form and notion of God acceptable to us. Thus, many are comfortable with God as the totality of natural laws and order which prevail in creation, and some others may find that natural creations and phenomena (sunset, starry skies, moonlit ocean, mountains) cleanse their mind and make them feel connected to totality. However, most people need to rely upon the concept of a more personal God for unburdening themselves as well as for promoting humility and many other finer and gentler emotions which worship brings to the forefront.

This is some of the preparation for Vedanta which we have to begin working on if this knowledge is to be meaningfully further pursued.

Incidentally, one may justifiably ask at this stage about the kind of preparation which deeply distressed or traumatized people are likely to need to be able to benefit from

Vedanta. As we saw earlier, a healthy ego, a level of morality and humanity, and some amount of intellectual capacity and maturity are required as preconditions for the serious pursuit of Vedanta. Vedanta deals with *normally abnormal* people! Others would certainly find consolation and healing in the process of preparing for Vedanta (including faith in and worship of God), but that is no substitute for expert professional help from doctors, psychiatrists, social-service organizations, or whoever else they may need depending upon the nature and severity of their individual problems.

We have now seen that the lessons that prepare us for Vedanta are really a way of leading daily life, finding space within us to handle our own emotions, and having the time and ability to analyze and do some introspection on experiences of our own life. For some, then, this preparation opens the door for the core teachings of Vedanta. This process is not rigidly sequential—it is neither necessary nor even possible to complete all preparatory types of learning before graduating to the so-called core teachings. All kinds of learning from Vedanta (and life) continue through all stages. However, some minimum preparatory change in orientation is needed if an individual mind is to become receptive to further learning.

Core Teachings

The core teachings of Vedanta can be looked at under three distinct areas:

- The real nature of you, the individual, who is the subject and for whom everything else in creation (including other individuals) is an object;
- The real nature of the rest of creation, which is an object for you, the subject; and
- The actual relationship between you and everything else in creation.

We will restrict ourselves to looking mainly at the first area: the real nature of you, the individual. Even in this circumscribed area, we will not look at everything that Vedanta has to say. This is partly due to reasons of size and space. It is more so because all these areas are ultimately interrelated and, therefore, it is not possible to deal fully with any one area without extending our scope to the other areas. On the other hand, what we are going to deal with should be easier to relate to and understand, because we will concentrate on that one area we know the best: our own self! By doing this, it is hoped that a better feel of the actual process of unfoldment of the teachings in a limited area is obtained as against a superficial overview of the whole mass of teachings.

The core teachings pertaining to the nature of our individual self can make some sense and become actually useful to us only if we have come to the firm conclusion that the entire approach of gaining something or becoming something is not an answer. Anything which is achieved extracts a price in terms of time, effort, and something else necessarily given up; effort and fear are involved in protecting what we have achieved because whatever has been achieved can, by its very definition, be undone; no achievement, however great or lasting, solves the subsequent problem of wanting more of the same thing or wanting something else. In fact what we want in the final analysis are not achievements, possessions, or absence of what we dislike—what we really want is a sense of satisfaction and completion, a sense of a pleased self within us. This is the real motivation behind all our actions, whether they are based on desire or fear. This is one of the broad, sweeping, and startling truths of our nature which the Upanishads provide—that wealth is not dear to us for the sake of the wealth but only for the sake of the pleased self; that a spouse is not dear to us for the sake of the spouse but for the sake of the pleased self; that a son is not dear to us for the sake of the son but for the sake of the pleased self; that in fact anything is dear to us not for its own sake but for the sake of our own pleased self.[11]

This truth holds good in cases of even apparently selfless action. So a soldier who bravely lays down his life for his nation does so because his strong patriotism is such that retreat and cowardice would inhibit a sense of a pleased self within him. Or a saintly person who spends her entire life amidst hardship and suffering to look after the poor and the diseased does so because she can experience a fulfilled sense of self only in this occupation and not in, say, running a business.

This truth does not condone our usual type of selfishness, wherein the crux is not only doing what pleases ourselves but also ignoring our duties and other peoples' rights in the process; nor does it devalue patriotism or saintliness because most of us find only narrower and more personal desires coming to the forefront. In our pursuit of security and pleasure we do often forget our duties, trample on the rights of others, and ignore our more selfless impulses. We do all this only to experience a pleased self; where we go wrong in such instances is to mistake a shallow and transient experience of pleasure as a substitute for true and lasting self-fulfillment.

Whatever may be our specific motivation in a given situation, the general fact remains that all our actions are related to doing something which is expected to lead to an experience of a pleased self. So, with this input from Vedanta (and after being convinced of its truth by our own experience and thinking) we can stop concentrating purely on external matters (possessions, relationships, pastimes) for our happiness and begin to look at the true nature of ourselves, because the self seems to be the locus of our true happiness.

---

11. *Atmanastu kamaya sarvam priyam bhavati—Brihadaranyaka Upanishad* 2.4.5

But before we get into the true nature of our own self, there is one more step of analysis which we need to carry out to better understand our desires and happiness. Our desires and the objects that apparently bring us happiness (or unhappiness) are infinitely varied and numerous. It is difficult to draw some general conclusions from this unordered mass. Vedanta brings in some order and facilitates our task by pointing out that all our desires fall into one of only three basic categories. All individual desires are really related to three primal urges common to all human beings. These are the urge to live, the urge to know, and the urge to be happy. Let us briefly look at each one of these fundamental impulses which, if frustrated, obstruct the sense of a pleased self within us.

A very large number of our desires and attendant actions are propelled by the basic urge to protect and prolong life. To want to live is a natural instinct in all living organisms, and human beings are no exceptions. Human beings exhibit this urge in a whole variety of actions, such as taking vitamin pills, wearing seat belts, doing a physical workout, eating sensibly, storing food, building shelters, eradicating germs, trying to predict cyclones, and so on. From the first gasping breath and suckling action of a newborn to the last gasping breath of a dying old man, the struggle first and foremost is to live. When we are capable of looking after ourselves and are in reasonably good health, we tend to forget the strength of our need to be alive. However, if the prospect of death makes even a small gesture at us (in the form of a potentially serious disease or a physically threatening situation) then a whole load of other matters, which then miraculously seem trivial, drops off from our shoulders! Nobody wants to die; everyone wants to live for one more decade or one more year or one more day or even one more hour! (One might ask what happens in instances of suicide or where an incurably diseased person chooses euthanasia. Here too, the basic urge to live never disappears but is overpowered by another equally fundamental urge to be happy. Death is welcomed by a few people when they have absolutely no hope of happiness; give them back their hope of happiness and death will be rejected.)

This urge to live is the urge just to be, to exist. In Sanskrit the word for existence is *sat*.[12] We all always want to exist or to be. However, this is obviously not all that we want. If existence were the only thing of consequence then the wayside rock, which could be a few million years old, should be our ideal!

This brings us to the next basic urge, which is the urge to be conscious, to be aware, to know. We do not want to be a million-years-old rock, because we do not wish to be inert. We would not choose a state of indefinite sleep even in the greatest possible luxury. We want not only existence but conscious existence where we have awareness, where we can know things. The basic awareness instinct is expressed in our need to know. This fundamental urge is the basis for effort towards discoveries, learning new things, grabbing the morning newspapers, not missing the 9 o'clock news, craning our neck to see when we hear a screech of car brakes, feeling restless till we ferret out a secret which our friend is trying to keep, and so on. The need to know is a facet of our awareness; it arises because consciousness is basic to us. The Sanskrit word for consciousness is *chit*.

The last primary urge within us is the urge to be happy or, really, to be unlimited. The Sanskrit word for happiness

---

12. It is not a coincidence that the word *satyam*, which means *truth*, is derived from *sat*—only something which really exists can be the truth. Further, it needs to be borne in mind that the translation of *sat* as *existence* is, as is true in the case of many Sanskrit words, just its closest possible approximation in a single English word; *sat* really implies an uncreated existence which is imperishable, timeless, and all-pervading and is the very ground of all other apparent being.

is *ananda*. We can have *sat* and *chit* but these do not mean very much without *ananda*. So, a terminally ill patient may choose to have life ended if the prospect of continuous pain permanently excludes ananda, or an infatuated lover may decide to commit suicide if he sees no prospect of ananda because being with his beloved is no longer possible. It is important to understand that ananda or happiness here is not restricted to laughter or to a "high" or to a state of bliss. It has a meaning closer to a sense of fullness where we are basically at peace with ourselves and with all and everything around us. It is a state where we are quite content to let things, events, and people be as they are—we might try to bring about some changes, but our inner sense of fullness or completeness is not limited by the results of our efforts in making those changes. In other words, when we are truly happy we can have preferences, but none of them are binding.

Vedanta tells us that all our wants and desires are finally aimed at obtaining a sense or experience of a pleased self within us. And this can happen only if the fundamental urges for sat, chit, and ananda are met in full measure at all times and in all situations. Nobody wants to exist only intermittently or for some limited time; nobody wants any boundary on their capacity to be aware and to know; nobody wants happiness only at one time of the day or only with one set of people or only in one location. It is very clear that our usual approach and actions will never result in full and unchanging sat, chit, and ananda. No amount of money or healthcare has brought immortality for any one of us. There is no way in which we are ever going to know all that is known to humankind (not to mention an infinite amount of the unknown but potentially knowable). Happiness, of course, is very ephemeral and requires a combination of things which must coexist before it is experienced. An experience of happiness requires a certain state of body, a certain frame of mind, a certain physical situation, and also a certain attitude from people around us. These combinations do not always take place as we want them. A variety of well-cooked, favorite dishes provides no happiness when one is trying to lose weight. A magnificent sunset or a beautifully tended garden provides no joy when we do not even see it because our mind is far away in mentally unraveling some business problem. The picnic could have been great fun—if the sun had not been so hot and if the flies and ants had stayed away. The new car seems to lose some of its glitter as soon as the neighbor gets a bigger and better car. There is no possibility of basking in warm congratulations on the completion of our learned book when we are amidst a group of persons who seem to be interested only in stock-market movements. Many things must work together to provide us happiness, and most of these are out of our control.

Further, our need for happiness is not restricted to the present. We can be deliriously happy right now if we have the love of a wonderful person. But it will not be long before we start worrying about the future security of this love and begin asking "How do I ensure that things do not change in the future? Will there be any competition? What will happen when I lose my youth (or money or whatever else)?" We do not even stop here in trying to feel happy. There are times when we go back to *past* unhappiness! "Why were my parents the way they were? Why did that friend betray me even though I had been so fair to him?" There is just no way in which we can obtain and retain full and permanent happiness.

If all this is so, then it seems impossible to continuously abide in a state where nothing inhibits the sense of a pleased self within us because of a full measure of sat, chit, and ananda at all times. Two possibilities exist here. Either we are looking for something which is impossible here and now (we do not know whether or not this state may occur in heaven!) or, alternatively, we are looking for what we want in the wrong way at the wrong place. Vedanta comes in here again to emphatically declare that our quest is neither for something impossible nor for something non-existent. It clearly states that it is possible on this earth and in this lifetime to abide in a pleased self because of sat, chit, and ananda in full and permanent measure.

And we all do have experiences of that special kind of fullness, however fleeting those experiences are. Some of us have been completely lost in beautiful music or a sunset. Some others have experienced unalloyed joy in holding a tiny baby. Yet others have been transported to virtual divinity when in deep love. In all these experiences, the real joy is the disappearance of the experience of our usual self which feels small, limited, and insecure. In ordinary experience we see ourselves as limited by our individual body, our individual emotions, and our individual intellect. There are obvious limitations to any individual body and mind. With our limited individual resources it is a daunting task to deal with an infinitely larger, more complex, and more powerful universe. Hence we feel small, limited, and insecure. In spite of this, we momentarily manage to derive a different kind of joy on those special occasions—music, sunset, infant, love. In these moments we lose our sense of individual limitation not because our mortality, lack of knowledge, and unhappiness actually disappear but because we briefly lose our sense of individuality itself and, with it, any sense of lacking.

The fact that happiness is experienced when the sense of individuality temporarily disappears may sound strange, but it is true. When we are truly lost in a trance of music, we are never aware of ourselves as an individual enjoying the music. Our individuality returns as soon as those magic moments end and we think back about our enjoyment—our thinking about any experience is always in the past, even though that past could be as recent as a fraction of a second ago. As soon as we become aware of ourselves as experiencers, the actual experience is already in our memory (however recent), and this is when comparisons with the past and concerns about the future start. This is true of all our experiences. The only difference is that in the usual day-to-day experiences, the stepping in of individuality after every moment of an experience is almost instantaneous, while in some special experiences (like being in a trance of music) there is a noticeable interval of time before our sense of limited individuality regains its hold. That is why such experiences show us, even though very briefly, how it is to feel the fullness, the joy, the sense of completeness when our usually perceived notion of a limited self is not present.

In a different way, the daily experience of deep sleep (the dreamless portion of sleep) also releases us from our sense of individuality and limitation. Deep sleep is the same for the king and the beggar—the beggar's sense of limiting poverty does not exist in deep sleep. Even a person who has become blind loses the limitations of blindness in that state. Sleep is desired and restful not only because it provides respite for the body but also because it provides respite from our sense of individual lacking or limitation. This respite is so pleasing that nobody complains that they need to sleep every day!

However, sleep is not the answer to our fundamental problem; if this were so then drink and drugs would be better substitutes for Vedanta, and death would be our most desired achievement. Our task is not to prolong a stupor wherein our problems do not intrude because our mind is temporarily unavailable. The reason for this is that as soon as our mind becomes available again (when sleep is over, or the drink or the drug wears off), the sense of limitation connected with our individuality comes flooding back, and often with greater vigor. Death is certainly not a solution, because if we, who have the problem of limitation in the first place, cease to exist then for whom does this solution have any relevance? We cannot win a game by opting out of the game! Attempting to destroy our individuality is also not the answer—even assuming that such a feat were possible, can one imagine living life like an animal or a programmed robot without the uniquely human aspect of individuality? As we will see later, our real task is to understand and see that the limitations of our individuality in no way affect our true nature, which is much greater than our individuality.

Let us go back to the possibility that the underlying desire for a full and permanent measure of sat, chit, and ananda may never be capable of actual fulfillment. Here, we need to rely upon our knowledge, based on our own observations and experience, that there is no need, no hunger, and no desire in nature without a corresponding means of its fulfillment. Just as hunger presupposes bread, so does our longing for total fulfillment presuppose such fulfillment. The urges to exist, to be conscious, and to be happy, permanently and without limitation, are universal and instinctive for all human beings everywhere and at all times. They are natural and do not have to be learnt or copied from others. It does not seem reasonable to dismiss them as invalid or incapable of fulfillment.

Supported by everyone's occasional and transient experience of freedom from a sense of individual limitation and supported also by the general scheme of nature, wherein no basic urge exists without the possibility of its fulfillment, Vedanta asserts that our goal of abiding in full-ness with a pleased self is neither invalid nor impossible. This then leaves the only other possibility, which is that so far we have been looking for this goal in the wrong manner at the wrong place.

Because we are all born with a limited body and a limited mind, our natural tendency is always to look outside of ourselves for reducing our limitations. We look for ways to prolong our life, increase our knowledge, and accumulate things expected to provide happiness. Our tendency to look outwards is reinforced by our perceptive senses which, by their very nature, are outgoing and outward-looking. But no scheme, no possession, no becoming ever works on our sense of limitation except temporarily, for reasons that we have already seen. Vedanta teaches us that after having reasonably exhausted the potential of things outside us to provide fundamental and final answers, it is now time to turn inwards.

But what does this turning inwards mean? Should we continuously watch our mind in an attempt to nip unhappiness in the bud? Should we give up all liking and preferences so that there is no possibility of disappointment and unhappiness? Should we work on developing a quality of thinking that can dull the sharp edges of every unpleasant situation by quick rationalization? ("If I do not have shoes, let me look at those who have no feet" or "Even though I dislike him, there must be something likeable in him because his mother likes him!") Clever attempts to think positively do not work, because as surely as night follows day, an opportunity for negative thinking will follow. We may tell ourselves that it does not matter that we do not have a Ferrari because we are blessed with a loving wife, but this will work only till we see someone who not only has a Ferrari but also a beautiful and a very obviously loving wife! Continuously watching our mind or attempting to stamp out likes and preferences involves continuous effort and tenseness because it is an unnatural struggle in a losing battle. Anything that involves effort, anything that involves change, anything which is becoming something other than what we already are can never be a solution.

We learn from our experiences with things of the external world that we will never achieve infinite and eternal sat, chit, and ananda by our finite and time-bound efforts. Efforts can take us a long way and are absolutely essential for several preparatory matters, but can never take us to the boundless and to the unchanging. We have now, by using our experiences logically interpreted in the light of Vedanta, painted ourselves in a very small corner where only one possibility remains. And this is one of the great and shining truths we are led to by Vedanta: that the true nature of our own self *is* sat, chit, and ananda here and now, for every one of us. This is the only possibility which excludes any effort, any change, any becoming—because what can be required to become what we already are?

This teaching of course provokes a flood of questions, doubts, and derision. Such a reaction is perfectly understandable because we certainly do not know ourselves as abiding in a state of fullness with no concerns about mortality, lack of knowledge, and lack of happiness. In fact our experience is exactly the contrary, and any claim that the true nature of our own self is sat, chit, and ananda in full and permanent measure has to be viewed with some cynicism and skepticism. Vedanta then has teachings to explain the fundamental ignorance with which each one of us is born, which creates this apparently contradictory state. After this, Vedanta moves into its real function of dispelling that ignorance.

Why do we all, without any exception, start with the fundamental mistake that we are small and limited if our true nature is sat, chit, and ananda? This fundamental mistake is not a mistake in the sense of an avoidable error. Nor is it punishment for some mythical "original sin." It just is a perfectly natural initial state of being, and shedding this ignorance is a matter of our growth as human beings. It is exactly like a baby being born physically incapable, emotionally immature, and intellectually undeveloped and then growing and learning to be a fully developed adult. We also need to grow out of our initial ignorance about our own self by intelligent effort and perseverance.

We have only our body and mind with which to receive inputs, analyze them, and enact our responses. All our activities of knowing, feeling, thinking, and acting are automatically circumscribed by the limitations of our natural equipment. Even if there were only one single human being on this earth, who would then have no conditioning because of others and have no knowledge of human death, that person would still feel limited because their capacity to know, feel, and act would be limited. There is no way of understanding and resolving the universal human experience of limitation without the knowledge of Vedanta because our limited body and mind can never discover the unlimited on their own. The question of how Vedanta itself first got this knowledge is an interesting *Chicken or egg first?* type of question, which has an answer but is outside our scope here. All we need to know at this stage is that Vedanta identifies this natural mistake as the root cause of all our fundamental problems and then proceeds to tackle the ignorance of the true nature of our own self.

How does Vedanta tackle this ignorance? In Vedanta, ignorance is beautifully compared with darkness. We cannot remove darkness by pushing it out—we can only dispel darkness by bringing in light! Ignorance is exactly like this: it can be removed only by the light of knowledge. Centuries-old darkness (say, in a sealed pharaoh's tomb) can be dispelled in a single instant by bringing in a light. And knowledge dispels ignorance no matter how old it is.

Our ignorance of the true nature of our own self starts with the most elementary mistake when we take ourselves to be our physical body. Our language is replete with this mix-up: we constantly use phrases like *I am tall, I am fat,*

I am dark, and *I am not well.* All these are of course attributes of the body which we identify with our own self when we use the pronoun *I* instead of the noun *the body.* However, our confusion is shown up by the same language when we point at a dead body and somberly pronounce "He is gone." If an individual is truly the body then no one can go anywhere till the body is present. Even more convincingly, we know that our sense of existence (the knowledge that *I am*) is not affected when parts of our body are affected. If we are the body then our sense of *I am* must reduce when, for instance, a limb is amputated. However, that doesn't happen; as long as we are alive, our knowledge of our own existence or our sense of being undergoes no contraction at all. Lastly, there is the impeccable logic that anything which we can be aware of, which is an object in our awareness, can never be us. If we are the body then how can we be aware of its size, shape, and other attributes? Just as the eye can never see itself directly as an object in its own vision, we could never have our body as an object of our awareness if we ourselves were, in fact, the body.

The logic that we have used to see that the body is not our true self is not as obvious in the case of the mind, but it applies equally well. We cannot be our emotions, because *we* are aware of them—we know that our mind is happy or angry. Similarly, *we* are aware of the varying states of our intellect—we know that our thinking is fuzzy early in the morning or that on a particular day our intellect is razor-sharp while on some other days it is dull. We, therefore, cannot be the intellect.

It is even more difficult to get over the notion that we are our ego. (We must be clear that by the term *ego* what is meant is not a sense of pride but, rather, that facet of our mind which gives us a special sense of individuality, which makes each of us feel that we personally are the doer or

knower or enjoyer.)[13] We may understand that we are not
our body or our mind, but surely we are our ego! But this
too is not correct. It is easy to take the ego as our true self
because it is the very root of our individuality. But if we
really study and analyze the ego we will find that it is just
a product of the mind, just a thought. Because it is a
thought of self-referral or an *I*-thought, it seems that the
ego really is our true self. However, if the ego is indeed the
real and final meaning of ourselves, then it cannot ever
disappear, at least as long as we are alive. But we are all
aware of the absence of ego in our deep sleep; we are all
also aware of the absence of an individual *I*-thought when
actually in a trance of music or love, however briefly. If we
are the ego, then *who* is aware of the *absence of ego* in deep
sleep or in moments when our individuality is absorbed?
Because we are not the ego, the ego can come and go;
because the ego is not the true nature of our own self, it is
available for us to be aware of.

If we are truly neither the body nor the mind (including
the ego), then are we some kind of combination of body
and mind? This too does not stand to reason. If the body
and the mind separately are not us, how can they become
us in combination? Further, they continue to be objects of
our knowledge separately as well as in combination and
therefore they can never be our true essence. But then what
are we as individual human beings?

Vedanta teaches that the true nature of each and every
one of us is self-evident consciousness. The statement that
the real nature of the self of any human being is self-evident
consciousness is very fundamental. Without fully understanding and totally accepting it, there is not much point in
going any further into Vedanta's core teachings. What we
need to recognize first here is that the true nature of our
own self is consciousness. We then have to see that this

---

13. The Sanskrit word for ego is *ahankara*, which literally means *I-maker*.

consciousness is in the nature of sat, chit, and ananda—
that is, of an unlimited and permanent nature.

What is actually meant by the statement that our true
nature is consciousness? We have already seen that when we
talk about an *I* we are not referring to our body, emotions,
intellect, and ego. But then what is this *I* which is our true
self? This is a natural question and we expect an answer in
the normal mode. We want to know a thing and we would
like to have it brought before us on a dissecting table so
that we can study and analyze it. This approach works very
well for something which *can* be an object in our awareness, but can never work for knowledge of our own self.
Our true self can never be a thing or a concept which can
be brought before us to study and analyze. If we are to
know our self in the usual manner of knowing, then who
would be the knower of this knowledge? If the knower is
different from us then our search for knowledge of self
cannot stop at a self as we know it at any time; it must logically proceed to *knowing that knower* because that would
be the real *I!* This regression can be carried on in an infinite
manner. If the knower and the object to be known are the
same then there cannot be any knowing as we understand it,
because knowing necessarily implies a knower separate from
the object to be known. Our search for self-knowledge can
stop only at something which cannot be known but which
just is. We can never *know* our true self in the conventional
way of knowing objects and ideas, because we are talking
about knowing the knower who is us. An eye cannot see
itself, because it itself is the means of vision. In the light of
our real nature, which is consciousness or awareness, we
can know everything else but never our own self.

Where does this take us? Do we conclude that we must
accept consciousness as the true nature of our own self
merely because someone says so? Of course not! This
would make Vedanta into a body of beliefs and dogmas,

which it is not. If the true nature of our own self is consciousness in whose light we become aware of everything,
then this consciousness itself should be self-conscious or
self-aware or self-illuminating. Just as a source of light does
not need another source of illumination to exhibit itself
because it is self-shining, consciousness has to be self-
evident. And self-evident it is, to each and every one of us!
We are all aware of one thing for the knowing of which we
need no inputs from outside, about which we never have
the slightest doubt, and which never changes at all during
our journey from birth to death. This is the knowledge of
our own existence, of our being. This is the knowledge *I am*.

Though this truth may seem somewhat insubstantial and
difficult to grasp, it is very important; as human beings this
is the only real capital we have to hold on to in our spiritual venture. We of course have a lot of other resources—
such as God, dharma, wisdom from books and people,
perseverance, intelligence, and so on—but all these are
concepts. Concepts by their definition are a product of
thought and are affected by our state of mind as well as by
our surroundings and conditioning; they are subjective and
capable of many interpretations. The concept of God varies
for different people; what constitutes dharma in a particular
situation is a matter of interpretation; what is wisdom to us
may be meaningless chatter for our neighbor; everyone's
notion of what is perseverance and intelligence is different.
These concepts are valuable and have their place but they
are not substitutes for that bedrock sense of personal existence which can never be denied, which is never affected by
surroundings or opinions, and which never needs external
confirmation or reassurance.

What is the sense that we are trying to capture when we
use the words *I am?* We must be careful not to mix this up
with extensions which effortlessly attach themselves to *I
am*. Here we are talking about awareness in the nature of a

sense of presence, as against the association of that sense of presence with a specific body and mind combination. We usually never stop at *I am* as just *am-ness,* but always think in terms of *I am John* or *I am a man* or *I am well* or *I am happy.* However, the meaning that we want to get and understand here has much more to do with *am* and not so much with *I.* If someone were to ask us "Do you exist?" and to this admittedly silly question we truthfully replied "Yes," what would we be referring to? We would be referring to the fact of our own existence, which is self-evident to us and which is in no way connected to a vision of our face, to our name, to our age, to our gender, or to our physical or mental health. If someone had asked us the same question twenty years ago, not only would we have given the same answer but we would have been referring to the *same* sense of existence, which has never been affected by subsequent changes in our age, appearance, occupation, and, perhaps, even name.

That sense of existence is our true self, and this is self-evident to us—we do not have to use memory, thinking, or judgment to know of our existence, nor do we have to rely on the evidence of our sense organs to confirm our existence. Our name, our body, and our mind are really not us but additions to our true self. We existed as infants before we were given a name and before we started responding to that name. Our basic existence continues unchanged through physical and mental changes. We never feel that some other being was us in our childhood, even though we have changed dramatically since then.

If this is so, then we need an explanation about why we never perceive ourselves simply as conscious beings but as personalities with several attributes (*I am John, I am a man, I am angry,* and so on). For understanding this we must first recognize that all our individual perceptions and thoughts are not the products of pure consciousness as such, but rather are the products of consciousness as reflected by the mind. In some ways this is similar to light, which is never directly visible but becomes apparent only when it reflects off some objects (including dust particles in the atmosphere). The human mind, by its very nature, can work only by creating dualities. For perceiving, judging, deciding, and acting, the mind works by creating a subject-object relationship. The mind has to take on the role of a subject which then perceives, comes to a judgment, and acts in relation to an object. This division (which is perfectly natural and necessary for living in this world) is really the source of the ego. The ego is nothing but the mind in the role of a subject for which everything else then becomes an object. Further teachings of Vedanta, beyond our scope here, go into a detailed analysis of this subject-object division. They lead us to the conclusion that we are only pseudo-subjects whose sense of individuality is a superimposition on our fundamental truth of unchanging, boundless consciousness.

The sense of being the subject (a separate individual), which is necessary for the mind to work and help us to live in the world, gets reinforced by our way of living and by our conditioning. The process of ascribing more and more importance to the initially utilitarian nature of the ego begins very early in life. We all casually note that a very young child starts vocalizing its individual wants by saying "Baby hungry" or "Jack wants chocolate" but then shifts to saying "I am hungry" or "I want chocolate." This is a vital shift from a functional individuality to a growing association with the ego. Embedded in the reality of our existence, the ego grows by using the resources of the rest of the mind and by drawing further fuel from our surroundings. Our current social setup, which has discarded many mechanisms that fostered humility, moderation, compassion, and lack of aggression, really excels at fanning individual egos.

While none of us chooses to have an ego, nor is it something evil by definition, the ego does bring about two important consequences, which cause several problems. The first consequence is that the ego covers the true nature of our own self, which is just simple, conscious existence. We all see traffic lights only as red, amber, and green not because that is the color of the real light but because the light is completely covered by a colored glass and the color of that glass is taken to be the color of the light. Similarly, the real nature of our true self gets hidden and the attributes of the ego are taken as attributes of the self. Instead of recognizing that our truth is consciousness which is currently *associated* with an individual body and mind structure, we begin to look upon ourselves as *being* that body and mind complex. And an overgrown ego makes this natural error bigger and deeper, and thus more difficult to resolve.

The second consequence of the outsized ego is its addition of an impossible dimension to our basic needs. As simple, conscious beings where the ego is merely a useful facet of the mind, our needs are determined by the three primal urges, which we labeled sat, chit, and ananda. It is possible for such a being to go through life without drawing deep anger, anguish, and frustration from the inherent limitations of the human body and mind. For instance, there is something natural and simple in seeing death as the other side of the coin of birth. We all know and admire people who try to lead healthy lives and seek medical help when necessary but are able to accept the ultimate inevitability of death with courage, fortitude, and equanimity; we also know of others who are reduced to quivering and whimpering or to cursing fate at the slightest prospect of death. The natural urge to protect and prolong life certainly brings sadness in the wake of death, but does not necessarily carry with it a huge amount of terror, anguish, and remorse. One can see composure in animals such as the gazelles and zebras on the plains of East Africa, where they live with the big cats who hunt them for food every day; here, death is a perfectly natural event in the process of life and living. The extra resistance and grief that death causes amongst many human beings comes not from the natural urge to live but from the needs of the ego, which adds its own agenda to the basic urges of the body and mind.

Our egos are not the primary truth of our existence, which is simple consciousness; they are secondary creations which are much more unstable and insecure. The ego's fear of annihilation is, therefore, much greater and its struggle for survival is much more frantic and terror-driven.[14] When we do not look for our true nature beyond the ego, then naturally the problems and fears of the ego become our problems and fears.

As we have seen earlier, egos derive their existence from a sense of individuality, from the notion of being a unique subject in a world where everything else is an unconnected object. When this notion of unique individuality gets larger than necessary, it sets itself up in competition, comparison, and hostility with other individual egos and the rest of creation. This is the real problem of duality. Instead of a simple urge to sustain life, this ego thinks in terms of using its cleverness and money resources to cheat death; the natural quality of awareness is now no more satisfied by just knowing what is necessary or what can be known: now there is a need to be seen and acknowledged as a well-informed individual; the urge to be happy gets completely

---

14. The point here is not to suggest that there should not be an attempt to survive or that there should be no concern about a painful process of death; the ego comes in the way of squarely facing up to the inevitability of death even after all due efforts to preserve life.

deformed and mutilated as soon as it passes through the lens of ego-driven individuality. Pleasures tend to go beyond the absolute and become more and more comparative. The enjoyment in owning and driving a car, for instance, is reduced when a neighbor gets a newer and better one; companions are sought not only for their ability to fulfill emotional and intellectual needs but also because they are the right sort of people to be seen with; a restaurant is chosen not only because of its food and ambience but also because it is the "in place" to go; possessions are sought and hoarded not only because they have great value in use but also because there is some kind of pleasure and security in being surrounded with possessions, as well as in the envy of other people; wealth beyond a point is sought not to meet any real needs or commitments but because of an overpowering urge to have an impressive score in the game of comparisons and one-upmanship.

Please remember that the purpose of saying all this is not to imply that the ego is some kind of cancer to be afraid of or to be banished; nor is it the intention here to imply that human beings are not capable of experiencing any natural, straightforward happiness because of the presence of the ego. The ego waxes and wanes, and its impact is different not only from person to person but also from time to time in the same person. Each one of us experiences uncomplicated happiness and fullness not only in a trance of music and love but also every time any of our desires are met—the ego only curtails the depth and length of these experiences and adds its own subjective overlays, such as pride of achievement or fear of loss. On the other hand, if we had no egos at all we would be no different from any animal. Animals also have primal urges to live, to know, and to be happy. The real difference is that while they know only those urges and act upon them as best as they can, we human beings are also aware of a special sense of individuality in addition to those urges. This special sense of individuality is the ego, and so when we describe a human being as the only self-conscious or self-aware being, we usually mean that the human being seems to be the only animal with an ego; consciousness or awareness of this ego is in common parlance labeled as self-consciousness or self-awareness. The ego is the veil which hides our essence of simple consciousness.

But, paradoxically, the ego is also the solution to our problem. Without the ego we could do no wrong (we do not consider animals as sinful even when they cause damage to us) but, by the same token, we could do no right as well. The uniqueness and the potential for inner growth in a human being lies not in eliminating the possibility of doing wrong but in doing the right thing when it is possible to do the wrong thing. There is no real freedom unless there is a possibility of misusing that freedom. Our special task as human beings is to use our awareness as individuals not only to fulfill our instinctive and ego-driven desires but also to see our larger reality. The ego, like any other part of creation, has a useful role to play; it only needs to be understood and given no more than its fair and objective value. Our ego is of and in the mind. Any understanding or any knowledge we are capable of as individuals is also of and in the mind. The mind is the locus of both the problem and the solution. Using the mind to transcend the mind is subtle and difficult; this is why there is so much confusion about self-knowledge. This is also why, although there is place for teachings and practices to bring down and keep the ego to a reasonable size, Vedanta never talks about totally annihilating the mind or ego or individuality.

Having digressed a little to look at the ego and its propensity towards covering our true nature, let us return to self-evident consciousness, which we said was the real essence behind all our individualities. We had said that this consciousness is self-evident to us in the knowledge of our own pure existence. We can call this sense of pure *am-ness* by its well-known Sanskrit label of *atma*.[15] The atma (self-evident consciousness) is our true self. What remains to be established is the sat, chit, and ananda nature of the atma, because our long search for fulfillment can end only if our real nature is sat, chit, and ananda in full and permanent measure. Or, to put it in different words, we have to understand ourselves as unchanging, boundless consciousness.

Let us begin with the *sat* aspect of the atma. *Sat* is existence, and we are looking for permanent and unchanging existence if our basic urge to exist is to be met. Something can be permanent only if it can never be denied in any period of time (past, present, or future). It can be unchanging only if it never changes irrespective of time, place, or situation. We have already seen that our sense of existence is neither changed nor affected when a limb is amputated or as we progress from young age to old age. Further, we can never say or feel "I do not exist," because who is then saying this or feeling this? No one can ever deny their own existence, because to do this, the denier must exist!

We may say that these arguments hold true only during an individual's lifetime. Can one not conceive of a time when one was not in existence (before birth) or of a time when one will not be alive? Surely one can do this, but only conceptually. A person can think of or imagine prior and posterior non-existence, but that is not an experience in reality. Witnessing our funeral conceptually is different from actually being present at our own funeral! (While we

---

15. Even after reflection, we do not usually reach a state of an impersonal *am-ness*, but have a sense of *I am*. There is already duality here because instead of just existence, there is an individual *I* aware of its existence. A technical and more precise term for this type of awareness is not *atma* but *sakshi chaitanya*.

are on this topic, it is interesting to note the working of our mind, whereby our future non-existence causes fear and concern but our prior non-existence does not seem to matter at all!)

Is there any other way of establishing the unchanging nature of the atma? Perhaps looking at our own experience of the death or destruction of anything may be of some help here. We all know that only things which have parts or attributes can undergo dissolution or change. Upon death, our body gets annihilated by breaking down into myriad chemical elements and compounds. During the course of our life, an attribute such as our beauty may change. Can such a fate ever befall consciousness? Does consciousness have parts or attributes for this to be possible? There is nothing in our experience which suggests that consciousness has any parts or attributes. In fact, it is because consciousness is partless that we have knowledge of parts. If consciousness had parts, we would need a second and partless consciousness to have knowledge of the parts of the first consciousness! Similarly, consciousness brings awareness of the attributes of other objects only because consciousness has no attributes of its own. (Here, we must be careful not to equate consciousness with intangible experiences like beauty or love. Because these thoughts and emotions are non-physical, they obviously do not have physical parts; however, they all have attributes, which make them changeable. Our experiences of beauty and love wax and wane, come and go; the consciousness by which we become aware of such waxing and waning or coming and going has to be itself without attributes.) Because consciousness is partless and attribute-less, it is reasonable to assume that it is not subject to death or any change.

Before we proceed any further in this discussion of the atma, we should bear two important factors in mind. The first is that we are looking at only a segment of Vedanta's core teachings in this book, which brings about its own limitations. The second and the more important factor is that, ultimately, no argument or discussion will completely establish the true nature of the atma. The atma is not an object or an emotion or a concept but is our very being, which is invariably present in all our sensing, emoting, and conceptualizing. While arguments have a role to play, one has to recognize their limitations in dealing with a reality which includes and goes beyond the mind. Our association with and attachment to our body is natural and immensely visceral. It is not surprising that the death of the body is taken as our death and that the concerns and fears of the ego are taken to be our concerns and fears. It is understandably difficult to accept that the end of an individualized and particularized set of physical and mental experiences does not have any bearing on the underlying awareness, which is unaffected by the death of any body. Really understanding the undying and invariable nature of the atma is a long, arduous, and subtle process which cannot be accomplished by a few words. In fact, when we truly and fully understand the eternal nature of the atma which is us, then Vedanta's task is done! Unfortunately, there are no shortcuts here. It would be very, very unusual to have real understanding of any aspect of the atma at this stage. For this understanding to become complete and established takes a lot more, including, as we have seen earlier, time, preparation, and the guidance of a teacher.

The *chit* aspect of the atma is relatively simple to deal with if we can look at awareness as just awareness, as against awareness of any specific object or concept. Awareness is an innate and obvious part of our existence. We are self-aware (our own existence is known) and aware in general. It is because of this awareness that we can read and understand these words, hear sounds, feel a touch, and have the sensations of smell and taste. It is this awareness which gives sentience and life to our body and mind. When this awareness aspect is no more apparent, we say that a body is dead, though its physical form may continue to exist. As a result of this awareness or consciousness we know what we know and also what we do not know! How else do we *know* that we *do not know* Sanskrit?

For individual human beings, awareness is manifested by the body and mind. In some ways it is like electricity being manifested by the movement of an electric fan; electricity does not fundamentally change, whether the fan works or stops, and not even when different fans work at different speeds. Similarly, specific knowledge or ignorance has to do with the working of specific minds and has nothing to do with basic awareness—one mind may know Sanskrit; another mind may not know Sanskrit but know that it does not know Sanskrit; and yet another mind may not at all know that there is a language called Sanskrit; and all this makes no difference to awareness. Even when we are not aware of our ignorance of Sanskrit (because we do not know that the Sanskrit language exists), we *are* aware of whatever we do know and we are also aware that we do not know anything *beyond* what we know! We are always aware! Awareness, like existence, is permanent and unchanging; it is self-evident and cannot be denied.

The last aspect of our true self which we need to consider is *ananda*. We have already seen that ananda is not so much laughter or a high state of bliss but more the sense of fullness and completeness. It is a state in which our peace and equanimity are not dependent on a change in or maintenance of some circumstances. A happy person is free to have preferences, and may also work towards their fulfillment. However, the actual results of their actions will not add to or subtract from their core of peace and fullness in spite of passing ripples of pleasure and displeasure on the surface of their personality. This can happen only if the person draws their basic happiness from a more fundamental and permanent source which is different from other objects and situations.

Let us look at a simple illustration to make this a little more vivid. Let us assume that you go to a restaurant for a simple meal and you ask for an orange drink, only to be told that the restaurant has nothing but colas. You have always preferred orange and you may decide not to have the cola at all, or go ahead and order the cola though it would have been nicer to have an orange drink. You have a preference for orange but it is not binding, and your peace of mind is not usually affected whether this preference is fulfilled or not. However, if you faced this same situation after having just lost your job or after a massive row with your spouse, you may become very annoyed because the restaurant did not have your preference, or you may get into further gloom and look upon the non-availability of your choice of a drink in a self-pitying way, as one more incident in fate's general scheme to keep you unhappy! This simplistic illustration is not to bring out the nature of ananda but only to make the point that our preferences do not always possess an ability to make us unhappy; a level of equanimity in the state of our mind is much more important.

We can have a sense of fullness and completeness when we need no addition, because we are already full. We can be full if nothing can be added to us. Nothing can be added to us only if we include everything or, in other words, if we are limitless. (If we are limited by any type of boundary then there must be something on the other side of that boundary which could be added to us.) So to be in the nature of full and permanent ananda, our true self needs to be limitless. The Sanskrit word for limitless is *ananta*—with a "t"—and this is at times used in place of the word *ananda*—the Upanishads describe the real self both as *sat chit ananda (existence, consciousness, happiness)* and as *satyam jñanam anantam (truth, knowledge, limitlessness)*.[16]

But how can we be limitless? This possibility is contradicted by our usual experiences, wherein our limitations are constantly reiterated. Here, too, we carefully need to segregate our body and mind combination from our true self in order to understand the ananta nature of the atma. What is ananta is the atma, and not any adjunct to it. Atma is the self-evident consciousness or awareness which is our very being. This awareness can be limitless only if it is all-pervading, which is the same as saying that everything must be contained within the atma.

This concept can be better understood by looking at the similarity of all-pervasiveness in the case of the concept of space. When we say we are in a room, we are also in space at the same time because the room itself is in space. We can go outward from the room to the building, street, locality, city, country, planet, solar system, galaxy, and the entire universe, and still have to say that each one of them is in space. This is because space is all-pervasive in the entire physical creation that we behold; because this entire creation is in space, there is no place in creation where space is not. Physical objects can exist only in space, but space can exist without physical objects. Further, space is not affected by any physical objects which exist within it. When we build four walls and say that the *inside* space is ours, this really has no effect on space itself; the division between *inside* and *outside* is purely notional and conventional. For the atma to be all-pervasive we have to see that everything is within the atma just as the entire physical creation is within space; we need to establish that there is

---

16. *Satyam* means *truth;* truth should be something which can never be denied, and so *sat* becomes *satyam. Jñanam* means *knowledge;* knowledge (including the knowledge that we do not know something) is an aspect of *chit,* and so *chit* becomes *jñanam.* As we have just seen, *ananda* comes from being limitless and thus becomes *anantam.*

nothing outside, beyond, or separate from the atma.

Something can be separate from anything else basically because of time or space. A pencil is separate from a telephone because they are separated by a distance in space; our younger age is separated from us by a distance in time.[17] For the atma to be separated from anything else by time or space, the atma itself must exist in time and space; this is really saying that time and space must be independent of the atma. However, this is not so; and this leads us to another startling truth: namely, that time and space only exist in and depend upon consciousness. Time and space only come into being when the chit aspect of the atma is fully manifested in our mind, and this happens only when we are both alive and not in deep sleep.

Let us look at our day-to-day experiences when we alternate between the states of waking, dreaming, and deep sleep. When we are awake, space and time certainly appear as independently determined quantities, unaffected by us. In fact it seems that, in our waking state, they affect us. In daily living this is a perfectly appropriate basis of looking at time and space, but that need not make this a true basis. It is also perfectly appropriate to look at the sun's apparent daily movements and enjoy a sunrise and a sunset, though the sun actually neither rises nor sets. We earlier referred to Albert Einstein's work, which has shown that at very high speeds the concepts of time and space lose their independent and fixed nature; they become a continuum and are dependent on the relative status of observers. Quite apart from modern physics, in our own personal experience we find time passing relatively more quickly when we are in a pleasant situation, and becoming almost unbearably slow when we are in unpleasant or boring circumstances. Our

---

17. Physical objects can be separated by space, time, *and* the characteristics of the object itself *(desh kaal vastu parichhinna)*: if we have a red car then the characteristic of redness excludes whiteness in the same car in the same space at the same time. However, here we are looking at atma, which is not an object and, therefore, has no attributes.

personal state of mind affects time as we personally perceive it. In our dream state we demolish the independently fixed nature of time and space even more dramatically—in a few hours while we are dreaming in bed, we may have traveled to a dozen different countries and seen our children grow from infants to adults! In deep sleep the entire concept of time and space completely disappears. We may use a familiar place and comfortable surroundings to fall asleep, but once we *are* in deep sleep, there is no notion of any place or space whatsoever. Similarly, we may be aware of time *up to* the very moment we fall asleep, but nobody can know the actual instant of time when they finally fall asleep because the very concept of time disappears when the mind no longer reflects the chit aspect of the atma.

We may argue that this does not make time and space dependent on us, because these concepts continue unchanged for others while we are asleep. Here again, we have to understand that our approach has been to restrict ourselves to looking at the fundamental problem of human beings from the viewpoint of a single individual. We have deliberately not extended our scope to look at the rest of creation. When we restrict our search in this fashion, we naturally go on the basis of our individual experience. Our experience is that we each have an individual kernel of consciousness within us; our experience of consciousness is not boundless but is confined to our body. While this experience is valid, it need not be completely true.

Our interpretation of any experience depends partly upon the limitations of our sensory apparatus and partly upon our perspective. If our eyes were capable of registering wavelengths beyond the visible spectrum of light, our experience of darkness would get modified to an experience of sight. If we look at space from the perspective of something which apparently encloses it—for example, a jar—then our understanding of space becomes compartmentalized. Such apparently individualized jar-space can be thought of as being available for storing something; if this jar is tossed up in the air, it would appear that the jar-space is tumbling up and down with the jar. However, from the more correct perspective of universal space, there cannot be any movement of space and there cannot really be individual jar-space because the walls of the jar are themselves in space.

Similarly, the understanding that the atma is beyond the concept of time and space requires a perspective which goes beyond the experiences of an individual body and mind. This is dealt with in the further reaches of Vedanta, which we have kept outside the scope of this book. Perhaps the only useful thing which can be said at this stage is that our experience of consciousness does not restrict our consciousness to any particular shape, size, or extent; something with no boundaries or delineation opens up the possibility of such a thing being beyond the ambit of space and time. (Here, again, we must not try to equate consciousness with shapeless concepts or emotions such as justice or love; these are just products of the mind, whereas consciousness is the substratum because of which the mind and its concepts become known.)

The fact is that the atma is *ananta* or limitless because it cannot be delimited. Any limitation involves separation, which needs time or space—but time and space exist only as concepts in consciousness and are dependent on it. A sword created by our mind in a dream cannot actually cut and divide us; time and space created by the mind cannot limit the atma, because the very mind and its functioning are dependent on the atma. What is limited is the body and the mind—they are both affected by time and space. What is limitless is the atma, and this makes it full because there is nothing outside its limits which can be added to it. Fullness is ananda, and so the atma is ananda.

We have now come to the end of a part of the core teachings which deal with the individual self and unfold the sat, chit, and ananda nature of the atma. I should clarify here that we have been looking at sat, chit, and ananda as three separate qualities. While this approach is useful for the purpose of analysis and initial understanding, in fact sat, chit, and ananda are not different qualities but just different ways of looking at the same thing. Sat is chit is ananda in any order! Further, *sat-chit-ananda* is not a description of the atma but *is* the atma (to some extent this is like saying that wetness, transparency, and liquidity are not descriptions of water but are water).

Even after all this is clearly understood, it does not solve our problem of being limited and wanting individuals who are afraid of death, who try to know as much as possible to conquer ignorance, and who desperately attempt to become happy! The problem is not solved, because some knowledge of the nature of the atma does not make us immediately feel the congruency between ourselves and the atma. With our conditioning and age-old habit, we almost instinctively consider our body and mind as our true self. Even as we read and say that the atma is really us, there is no experienced conviction of this truth. We still look upon the atma as an object to be understood and used by *us* even though this *us*, which we consider to be our real self, is nothing but our mind and ego. It is very difficult to know with feeling that we *are* the atma which cannot be thought of in the third person (as *the atma* or *this* or *that*) but as the truth of the only first person we know: *I*.

We can, perhaps, now get a feel for the difficulty in the teaching and learning of Vedanta. At the very beginning of the core teachings, we run into the problem of the inherent limitations of argument and conventional experience in understanding that our true self is the atma and then under-standing the true nature of this atma. Even though most students of Vedanta are able to accept fairly quickly that their true nature is not restricted to their body or their mind, it is not easy to accept that the consciousness which is their underlying reality is unfettered by time and space; after all, everyone's *experience* of consciousness is restricted to their own individual body, which is limited by both time and space. Further, while on one plane we may understand that the atma is our reality, this is not the same as knowing with full conviction that the apparent object of our under-standing (the atma) is the real subject: *I*. We continue to consider our mind and ego as the subject, at a conditioned and almost instinctive level. Our orientation towards getting, using, and becoming (which is vital in fulfilling our usual desires) becomes a barrier when it comes to just being what we already are. There has to be a fundamental shift in our usual way of thinking and understanding. This cannot be done overnight and by mere logic. Apart from special attributes (which we will look into in a later chapter), a lot more work and time, as well as practices such as meditation, are needed under the guidance of the indispensable teacher.

The effort and help of a teacher do not guarantee that full and abiding understanding will occur in a specific indi-vidual's mind. However, even if the full message of Vedanta may not appear for or appeal to a specific individual, there is immense benefit to be gained from just the fringes of Vedanta. A little work and reflection on the possibility that we are different from our body and mind can itself open up some valuable space inside us. We may begin to see that our sensations and emotions are happening only to our body and mind, with our real self being an unaffected witness of that body and mind; this may inhibit the usual process of taking instant personal delivery of those sensations and emotions. If we encounter an insulting personal remark, the usual thought is that *I* have been insulted and the knee-jerk reaction then is a hot flash of anger and, perhaps, a more insulting retort. If we can understand that the target of the insult is our ego and the tempting urge to react by anger and retort comes from the mind and ego, this permits the possibility of being a little more objective and of responding instead of reacting. A response may, on the face of it, be identical with a reaction if the situation so warrants, but the difference is that in a reaction we are helpless and driven, whereas in a response we are in control of our mind. Here, our intellect has a larger role than our emotions. Even if uncontrolled reactions continue to occur in the beginning, some teachings of Vedanta have a chance to work after the provocation is over, when one can look back upon the incident and learn from its negative emotions and actions. A small beginning in this direction grows quite rapidly because, like a vicious circle, this virtuous circle also becomes self-reinforcing. A little more objectivity, restraint, and balance encourages better understanding of the teachings and leads to behavior which tends to reduce provocative action from others. Everybody can utilize and benefit from even the limited teachings of Vedanta.

In what we have seen so far, we have by and large restricted ourselves to some teachings of Vedanta which are used to establish that the atma is our reality and that this atma is in the nature of sat, chit, and ananda. If this were the extent of Vedanta's teachings, it would not only leave many vital areas uncovered but would also create further doubts and confusion. If my atma is ananta—that is, limitless—and your atma is also ananta, then we have the absurd situation of two limitless things, and this, by definition, is not possible. If sat is the nature of my atma, where was it before my birth and where does it go after my death? Also, even if my atma is in the nature of sat, chit, and ananda, why does that exclude the possibility of a larger and more powerful reality—God—whom I must fear and who makes me feel powerless and insignificant in comparison? What we have seen so far is not only an incomplete picture; we have also, in some areas, stopped at dangerous half-truths. Vedanta's teachings go much further than what we have so far considered; not only do they deal with the doubts and questions just mentioned, but they take us on an extended journey which goes into an exploration of the rest of creation and then into the relationship between an individual and the rest of creation. Having seen the difficulty of dealing with even the beginnings of the core teachings which we have tried to touch upon in this section, there is no intention of getting any further into the actual teachings of Vedanta in this book. I will only mention that it is generally considered that Vedanta's core teachings are contained in the so-called *mahavakyas* or "Great Sentences."

We saw earlier that all the Upanishads belong to the end of each one of the four Vedas. Traditionally, one sentence is picked out from one Upanishad from each of the four Vedas, and so we have four mahavakyas. The most often quoted mahavakya is *tat tvam asi*, which means "You are That." This sentence is really in the nature of an equation where You = That, or where you are equated with the whole. This equation does not convey very much unless we have adequate background and understanding to begin with. The well-known scientific equation $E = mc^2$ may contain the explanation for the awesome power of a nuclear device, but will reveal the knowledge it contains only to a trained physicist. In Vedanta too, a lot of preparatory work is necessary for the mahavakya to yield its real meaning. And the greater the preparation and exposure, the more depth and subtlety will be revealed by the same mahavakya. In the You = That equation we have so far only looked at some of the *You* part to try to gain some understanding of the real nature of *You*. We have not at all gone into the *That* portion of the equation. *That* covers the rest of creation as perceived by any one individual.

An individual does not exist in isolation; each of us is confronted by and has to deal with the rest of creation. Any teaching which claims to remove fundamental ignorance cannot get far if it deals only with the reality behind an individual without dealing with the reality behind the rest of creation. Vedanta exhaustively deals with *That* and unfolds the true nature of the world that we behold. Different levels of realities (there is such a thing!) are explained, and the defects in our usual way of looking at things around us are corrected to bring about objectivity. Because *That* includes God, the teachings go into a deeply meaningful exploration of God.

The task of Vedanta does not stop here. Even before we study Vedanta, we know that we are different from the world and that we are not God. If Vedanta only explained the true nature of an individual and the true nature of the rest of creation, that would certainly be helpful, but not enough. Vedanta goes on to establish the identity and unity behind these two apparently widely different terms. This is a truly radical unity because it is not only unity behind different objects (such as protons, neutrons, and electrons being the common substratum of both gold and iron); it is the startling unity between the subject and objects, between the seer and seen. Vedanta now brings us to *advaita*—non-duality—and introduces the only fundamental reality, which it labels *brahman*.[18]

The appreciation of this non-duality underlying apparent differentiation between the subject and objects has mind-

---

18. The etymology of the word *brahman* provides some interesting insights. The Sanskrit root from which this word is derived is *brih*, which has connotations of both bigness and growth. Even though we use the word *big* as an adjective to qualify a noun, in fact the noun also qualifies the adjective—when we say "big mountain" and then say "big microbe," the nouns *mountain* and *microbe* affect the notion of bigness which is conveyed. When we use the word *big* or *bigness* without any noun, we can convey a notion of an unqualified or unlimited bigness; the word *brahman* conveys bigness in this immeasurable or all-pervading sense. The connotation of growth which this word conveys provides an interesting connection to present-day scientific thinking, wherein the entire universe is considered to be ever-growing or ever-expanding.

boggling implications. We started looking at Vedanta's core teachings by saying that the atma is neither the body nor the mind but self-evident consciousness. This is very much an apparent duality between what is atma and what is not atma. However, it seems that at the end of the teachings of Vedanta, we are led to a great unity. This seems very confusing. There is a further and greater problem. Advaita Vedanta is knowledge which needs a teacher, and thus promotes a duality consisting of the teacher and the taught; all knowing actually involves a triad of the knower, the object to be known, and the process of knowing! How can a body of knowledge dealing with ultimate unity rely upon a method based on multiplicity? Let us look at some other fundamental problems which arise from a non-dual truth. Does not advaita imply the doing away with any notion of individuality? If this is so then what happens to our individual free will, which permits us to choose and to act? Without individuality there cannot be free will and there cannot be any one who chooses to learn Vedanta or makes an effort in that direction. In a non-dual state who is to learn, who is to teach, and for what? How does a single fundamental reality leave any scope for differences between righteousness and sin, or even for a concept of God, which must include godly qualities and exclude ungodly ones? How and why does this unity become manifest in the multiplicity of creation that we can all behold? These are only some of the doubts and questions which arise as the pursuit of Vedanta goes further and deeper. We are, of course, not going to attempt to clear up any such problems here. The only hope is that the curiosity raised by even mentioning these matters will lead to further inquiry into Vedanta.

One last issue which may be useful to clarify here is the perplexing absence of emphasis on ethics and humanity in the core teachings of Vedanta. From this, one may falsely conclude that the Upanishads are, at least to some extent, amoral and that Vedanta is an abstract and self-centered construct with no particular concern for the rest of humanity. This wrong impression arises only if it is forgotten that the focus of the Upanishads is self-knowledge. In keeping with this focus, their concern with ethics, love, and compassion is limited to the contribution which such matters make to the goal of self-realization; in a way, the Upanishads are above these matters because, for them, things like morals are not ends in themselves but means to a different end. This, however, does not mean that Vedanta is a pursuit wherein ethics and humanity can be forgotten. In the scheme of Vedanta, the grounding in dharma (which encompasses both ethics and appropriate attitudes towards other beings) in the earlier and preparatory stages is taken for granted and it is assumed that there is no further need to emphasize proper conduct and healthy concern for fellow beings. After all, no scripture or writing can provide equal emphasis to all aspects of its subject. If any student of Vedanta, especially in the context of our present times, finds that they are deficient in these matters, it is up to the student and their teacher to supplement the wisdom of the Upanishads with lessons of rectitude and loving-kindness in daily life.

We will stop our look at a part of Vedanta's core teachings here and touch upon some other teachings which are interesting but should not be looked upon as constituting the vital heart of Vedanta.

Peripheral Teachings

An age-old body of wisdom which deals with fundamental questions of human existence has also to develop a peripheral set of teachings to deal with a variety of conditioning in and curiosity of different seekers. Seekers know their own individuality and the world as they behold

it to be the only truths; explanations for events and circumstances affecting individual lives and the world are needed
before they are transcended and a more fundamental
reality is recognized. Here we will look at only a few
representative areas of such peripheral teachings before we
move on.

Some of the questions about individual human lives
which commonly vex people are centered around the
theory of karma. This theory not only goes into the results
of good and bad actions but, further, leads to a concept of
the soul and its transmigration across individual lives. The
theory also provokes discussion on the perennial controversy between destiny and free will. The basic karma theory
is nothing but a theory of causality, which merely says that
every action causes an effect. This is self-evident, supported
by our everyday experiences, and needs no explanation.
However, the karma theory extends the results of any
action from the obvious to the not so obvious. The belief
here is that all actions produce visible or directly
connectable results *(drishta phala),* and also invisible
results *(adrishta phala),* in the sense of results which could
appear at a much later point in time without having any
obvious connection with the original action.

Actions in accordance with righteousness and some religious actions, such as prayer, may bring appropriate drishta
phala; an act of kindness by us may result in gratitude and
in a reciprocal act of kindness towards us, and prayer may
quieten our agitated mind, as direct results. These righteous
acts would also bring adrishta phala (called *punya* in this
case) in the form of some future good fortune, such as
winning a lottery or avoiding serious injury in a potentially
fatal accident. Wrong and prohibited actions would also
bring their appropriate drishta phala and adrishta phala
(the indirect results here are termed *papa*). The drishta
phala is easy to understand, because of obvious cause and

effect relationship, and easy to deal with, because results appear in a relatively short time. The adrishta phala comes in a much more mysterious way, because there is no discernible connection with any specific action; its effect can be more forceful, because the delaying of results to a much longer future time permits accumulation of adrishta phala from a large number of actions, which then collectively effect a single result.

We saw earlier that on the path of karma (as a part of preparation for Vedanta) a person could develop a more balanced attitude towards the actual results of an action of theirs by recognizing that their own action was never the only input: the final result would depend upon inputs from actions of several other people, natural events, and circumstances beyond the control and even the knowledge of the individual doer. The karma theory relates all these other inputs, through a very complex network, to the past actions of the doer and considers them to be the adrishta phala of such past and apparently unconnected actions.

Any mention of the karma theory leads to two immediate questions:

- Is there any proof for this theory?
- Does this theory remove the importance of current action on the part of any individual?

There is no acceptable proof of the existence of *punya* and *papa* as the adrishta phala of individual actions. At the same time, there is no way to disprove this theory—nor does it seem entirely illogical to admit the possibility of actions producing subtle and distant results in addition to apparent and immediate ones. If we consider some of the issues and possibilities that science is currently investigating at the level of subatomic particles and at the level of the heavenly bodies, we find that many of them are so radical and so contrary to any known logic that the possibility of actions having distant and apparently unconnected results seems almost tame in comparison. However, until there is better proof, we have to take this belief on faith—and only if we wish to. It is not necessary to subscribe to this belief as a condition for benefiting from Vedanta. One can go ahead quite comfortably without getting involved in the karma theory, on the basis that one should concentrate on solving the actual problems of the current life without wasting time in ascertaining the lineage of these problems or worrying about some unproven past and future lives which this theory brings in. However, if accepted, this theory answers a lot of questions; it also brings in a number of other beliefs in its wake.

If subtle results of present actions are going to bear fruits in the form of *punya* and *papa* for an unknown length of future time, then this belief is a very powerful force for promoting ethics and righteousness. Even if we can cleverly escape from immediate and obvious retribution for our wrong actions, we cannot escape from the *papa* it generates, which will come home to roost in an unpredictable manner at an unknown time; on the other hand, one can rely on the benefits of *punya* from righteous actions even though they may not be available right away.

What happens to the adrishta phala which has not borne fruit till the death of an individual? After all, if such results can come much later, then some unmanifested accumulation must remain at the time of death—if nothing else, then at least subtle results of actions carried out just prior to death should remain pending. Here we have the concept of a *sukshma sharira* (fine or subtle body), which is akin to the concept of soul in some other traditions. However, we must be very careful to note that this sukshma sharira, or soul, is *not* the atma—it is not the real us. The sukshma sharira is the potential life-force and the potential mind without which the physical body-mind structure of a human being would not be able to function. In its aspect as potential life-force, the sukshma sharira is like a bridge between the inert existence of the body and the existence of the atma, which is pure consciousness. In terms of an analogy, we can look upon the atma as a light and the body as a mechanism which comes alive only when energized by this light; to take this analogy further, let us assume that the mechanism needing light is placed in such a manner that light from the source can reach it only by means of a reflecting mirror. The sukshma sharira is like that mirror, without which the sensory and action capabilities of the body cannot be sustained.

In its aspect as the potential mind, the sukshma sharira is the subtle seed of mental faculties such as the intellect, the desires, and the sense of individuality.

The belief is that this subtle body joins the physical body at the moment of conception of an embryo and gives it life and individuality. It continues there until its death. When someone points at a dead body and says "He is gone," the reference is to the sukshma sharira, in whose absence the body, even though intact, is without life. The adrishta phala of actions are considered to accrue to this subtle body. While the physical body and the manifest mind of an individual get destroyed and lose their identity upon death, the subtle body subsists; it can be destroyed only by the fire of knowledge. Till the fundamental ignorance associated with each sukshma sharira is dispelled by complete and unchanging knowledge of the true self, this subtle body continues. Because this subtle body can continue beyond the death of the physical body, the unexpired or unmanifested accumulation of adrishta phala may bear fruit for that subtle body at any future time when it is associated with another physical body-mind complex.

Traditionally, adrishta phala in the context of a sukshma

sharira is seen as divided into three categories: *prarabdha,
kriyamana* (or *agami*), and *sanchita.* Prarabdha is that
portion of the accumulation of the unmanifested results of
a subtle body which comes to fruition during that subtle
body's association with a single physical body—during a
single human lifetime. It is the prarabdha (both *punya* and
papa) which determines the characteristics and the basic
circumstances of that individual—race, sex, build, basic
health/emotions/intellect, natural talents, family conditions, and so on. (Prarabdha explains a Mozart, who could
compose music at the age of five years, or a Ramana
Maharshi, who realized the truth and lived a life free of
fundamental ignorance without the benefit of any known
teacher or study of scriptures.)

Prarabdha continues to unfold during the entire lifetime
of an individual body-mind complex and affects every
detail. However, prarabdha is not the only factor which
has an impact during a life. An individual continuously
acts while living, and each action generates its own current
drishta phala and adrishta phala. This is called *kriyamana.*
Some of these results can become manifest during the
current life itself and may thus reinforce or nullify some of
the events and tendencies already at work in our life.
Therefore, this belief system and the acceptance of
prarabdha in no way implies embracing fatalism or helpless acceptance of the forces of destiny. Although there
is something like destiny which has some unchangeable
elements (our parentage, for instance) and which provides
some tendencies (for example, towards anger or cheerfulness) and some inclinations (such as towards science,
music, or spirituality), there is scope for present action
to have a determining influence in an individual's life. In
fact, tradition beautifully says that a wise person should
consider artha (security) and kama (all types of pleasures)

as things which can be partaken of without too much concern or effort because prarabdha has a large role to play here; however, dharma and moksha (liberation) are matters to be actively striven for without waiting for prarabdha to appear.

The entire stock of potential results available for a subtle body, just before its joining up with a new physical body, is termed *sanchita,* which is like an opening balance in the account of karma. Only a part of this opening balance actually comes into play during a single lifetime as prarabdha.

The karma theory goes into much detail about actions and results, and how they arise, get stored, and become manifest; the sukshma sharira and its transmigration across individual lives is also a topic by itself.[19] We will not get into the details of these matters here. I will only mention one interesting aside about the sukshma sharira before we move on. We all know that we mistake our body for our true self. However, this mistake does not seem to occur with other possessions which can also be very near and closely associated with us, such as an old watch or a favorite shirt. If our skin is brown, we identify ourselves with it by saying "I am brown"; however, if our body-hugging shirt is blue, we never even once feel "I am blue." Why does our notion of *I*-ness extend only to our skin and not a fraction beyond? The answer to this is that the sukshma sharira takes the exact shape of the physical body that it is currently associated with. As the sukshma sharira energizes the body with the reflected light of the atma, the sense of being alive extends to the limits of the body bounded by its skin and not to anything beyond. It is for

---

19. I should clarify here that the concept of transmigration of souls with their individual stocks of *sanchita* is relevant to an individual trying to understand the karma theory from the standpoint of their own individuality. At the end of the full teachings of Vedanta one gains a different perspective of individuality, which consequently modifies the understanding of the karma theory and the concept of individual souls.

this reason that the error of considering other things to be *I* does not extend beyond the boundaries of the body; it is for this reason that our *experience of consciousness,* which is limited by the extent of our senses, is always that of an individualized pocket of consciousness and not that of universal consciousness.

Let us now turn to teachings about the performance of rituals and the worship of various deities. A general impression of the Vedic religion is that it centers around complex ritual worship of a whole host of different gods and goddesses, with many of them appearing to be in startlingly grotesque forms. These divine beings are supposed to populate various hierarchical "upper" worlds (generalized as *svarga*, or heaven), while the "lower" worlds (*naraka*, or hell) are the residence of unsavory beings of different orders of evilness. It must be remembered here that though Hinduism and Vedanta are closely connected by history and culture, we cannot read all the teachings of the Hindu religion into Vedanta. Vedanta does not require anyone to accept the notion of any heaven or hell—it is Vedanta's commitment to lead a qualified seeker to freedom from fundamental ignorance *here and now* which makes it so different and special. Also, strictly speaking, Vedanta does not require us to worship any specific god or carry out any ritualistic practice; although for most people the psychological and emotional consequences of prayer are quite essential, this theoretically is still a matter of choice.

The colorful pantheon of deities is a combination of folklore and popular religion. Stylized versions of different divine qualities are depicted in the forms of different deities, providing a whole range of options from which to seek comfort and solace, depending upon an individual's emotional orientation. However, these forms have no real connection with Vedanta. The entire gamut of rituals contained in the earlier portion of the Vedas[20] also has no direct bearing on Vedanta except as some possible preparatory steps.

Similarly, the possibility of going to heaven (whose existence can be based only on belief, with no way of proving or disproving this concept) does not concern Vedanta. If heaven exists and can be obtained by righteous actions, it is another temporary "becoming," and all "becomings" (like becoming rich or becoming famous) involve finite effort for temporary results. One can always be displaced from any state which one can reach by effort. No finite effort can take us to the timeless and the boundless, which is Vedanta's objective—this can be done only by the removal of ignorance about our true, timeless, and boundless nature. Therefore, we can consider concepts of various gods, of rituals, and of heaven and hell as peripheral to Vedanta: they may be helpful to different people for different reasons to a different degree, but are not uniformly essential for understanding the teachings of Vedanta.

We can now look at portions of Vedanta which contain much material dealing with the creation of the universe. There is natural curiosity in us to understand when and how this entire creation began and where it is headed in the future. This curiosity is the basis of a lot of scientific effort. Current scientific belief (and I emphasize the words *current* and *belief*) is that our known universe began about fifteen billion years ago when an incredibly compact and dense kernel of all known matter erupted in a violent expansion (the big bang theory) which, over the aeons, has led to our far-flung universe, which is still expanding from its initial expansionary forces. There are no explanations about

___

20. As we saw earlier, the latter portion of the Vedas which contain the Upanishads is called Vedanta; the same latter portion is also known as *jñana kanda* (*knowledge section*). The earlier portions of the Vedas are often termed *karma kanda*, which means *action (or rituals) section*, wherein the objective is not knowledge but fulfillment of rightful desires.

where that first kernel of matter came from or how long this expansion will continue or what the boundaries of the universe are. In some ways this whole search is like the search of a figure in a dream trying to find out the material from which that dreamworld is made and trying to establish the boundary of the dream. Vedanta deals with the universe only as a dependent reality and relates it to that non-dual, fundamental reality called brahman; this is part of Vedanta's core teachings dealing with the *That* portion of the You = That equation. However, the detailed mechanics of creation are really peripheral and, rather than being final conclusions, are more of a model (out of many possible models) representing a view of the process of creation prevalent at a particular time.

Just as in a usual textbook of chemistry we have a list of elements which are considered basic in all matter, Vedanta lists five items which it considers to be the basic building blocks of creation: *akasha* (space), *vayu* (air), *agni* (fire), *apa* (water), and *prithivi* (earth). These elements are in ascending order from the subtlest (space) to the grossest (earth); each of these elements is related to one of our senses: space to hearing, air to touch, fire to sight, water to taste, and earth to smell. There is a description of a detailed process (termed *panchikarnam*) whereby the gross and subtle aspects of each of these five elements gets mixed in different proportions to produce the infinite variety of the tangible and intangible parts of our universe. These explanations are quite detailed; some portions are almost poetic, while others appeal to logic and may be supported by our current and future scientific discoveries. However, these matters are not critical to Vedanta's real teachings and one need not be overly concerned if some of them seem a bit far-fetched or incomprehensible.

To my mind a more important question in relation to the universe is not How? but Why? One answer to the question

"Why this Universe?" is the counter-question "Why not?" When we question creation as a whole, we are really questioning its creator or trying to fit his powers within boundaries of what we think he should do and what we are capable of understanding. As we ourselves are part of creation, this is a bit like a shadow wanting to understand why and how all shadows are created.

Another way to look at this problem is to consider whether this question can ever be really answered at the level at which it arises. We all know of that trick question (to be answered only in a *Yes* or a *No*) which asks "Have you stopped beating your wife?" Assuming that one has not been guilty of such reprehensible doings, this question can never be properly answered because the question itself has been framed in a defective manner. To know why this universe (which includes us) is created is really to know the purpose of the universe. To know the purpose of anything, we have to see it in a larger context. We cannot be part of a thing and hope to understand it; we must be able to stand outside and away from that thing to define its boundaries and understand its function. However, we, as individuals, exist only as part of the universe; while being this integral part of creation, how can we ever hope to know and understand creation objectively and from the outside? The question itself is defective and cannot be answered.

It is really a sign of the strength of our ego that such an egocentric question arises at all. And, in fact, questions about reasons for the existence of the universe or the purpose of life never occur to us in our truly happy moments, because during those times our sense of individuality temporarily vanishes. Actually, our real question is not "Why this Universe?" but "Why this struggle?" and this arises from the ego's ceaseless struggle to become sat, chit, and ananda, which (ironically) is the true nature of our own self.

We will now turn to another area which could be

considered peripheral to Vedanta. This relates to the practices of yoga. The word *yoga* really means to *join together (yoke)* or *to unite*, but over the years this word has become a catchall word to cover a lot of mystical-sounding activities. Without going into all the mysteries that the word *yoga* may be taken to mean, we will restrict ourselves to the recognized school of traditional practices and philosophy known by that name. The founder of this ancient school was the well-known sage called Patanjali, and his school is called *ashtanga* (literally, "eight-limbed") yoga because it consists of eight steps. So, when we talk strictly about yoga, we mean Patanjali's suggested practices, divided into eight sections, for bringing about a certain resolved state of the mind. Unlike Vedanta, yoga's emphasis is not so much on understanding and knowledge as on concentration and meditative practices whereby the mind reaches a stage in which the sense of individuality is fully absorbed and dissolved.

We will not get into the merits and demerits of Patanjali's full prescription, but just say that each of his suggested eight steps could be found useful in some context of Vedanta and could thus be considered peripheral to Vedanta. Patanjali's eight steps are: *yama, niyama, asana, pranayama, pratyahara, dharana, dhyana,* and *samadhi.* (Each of these steps has many substeps, which we will not detail here). *Yama* and *niyama* deal with self-control, values, and ethics. *Asana* deals with physical health and postures necessary to sit in undisturbed meditation for a long time. *Pranayama* has to do with a variety of breathing and breath-control techniques not only to make for a healthy body but also for a peaceful and collected mind. The next four steps are really to take a prepared body and mind into deeply meditative states for achieving yoga's real objective. As one can see, a Vedantic seeker could also use many of these practices, which produce a disciplined, alert, and collected mind. However, some of these practices (especially advanced meditation practices) do, in some cases, lead to mysterious experiences like unusual visions, sounds, smells, sensations, and feelings as well as the ability to demonstrate some supernatural powers. Whether these experiences merely arise from autosuggestions or not and whether these fascinating powers are real or not are debatable issues. In general, I have personally no difficulty in accepting that some strange things which defy our logic and understanding could happen in our phenomenal world. The universe is not only stranger than what we know—it is likely to be stranger than what we can know!

Be that as it may, these apparent visions and powers have very little to do with the true objectives of yoga (Patanjali himself warned his followers not to get carried away into tempting but useless sideroads) and certainly have nothing to do with Vedanta. In our pursuit of Vedanta we are at liberty to use such yoga practices as support our preparations and objectives but should guard against attempts to experience and wield peculiar visions and powers, which only build the ego, which are just another "becoming," and which actually delay addressing our fundamental problem.

I am going to touch upon one more area which is peripheral to the Vedantic pursuit and seems to generate some wrong notions. This is the topic of vegetarianism. It seems to be a belief in some quarters that Vedanta preaches vegetarianism and that to become a vegetarian is a precondition for this learning. This is not strictly true. Following a vegetarian diet has to be looked at in its larger context, which is *ahimsa (non-injury)*. *Ahimsa* is the cornerstone of Hinduism. If one statement captures the spirit of the Vedic religion, it is *ahimsa paramo dharma (non-injury is the highest form of righteousness)*. Vedanta also attributes much importance to ahimsa as a whole

approach and an attitude towards life in general, especially
in the preparatory stages. Here the emphasis is not merely
on eating vegetarian food but on non-injury in thought,
word, and deed. The point here is an attitude of doing the
least possible harm to all things in the process of living.

This attitude can genuinely arise only when one feels a
connection with and compassion for everybody and everything that one deals with. There is not much purpose in
being strictly vegetarian if our mind is generally filled with
hostility and our usual intentions are to harm others not
only by overt physical violence but also by words and
thoughts. Being a vegetarian is a logical extension of an
attitude of care, concern, gratitude, and love. The killing of
animals causes them obvious pain; there is no such obvious
suffering in the case of plants (we do not see tomatoes flee,
squealing in fright, as we pick them!).[21] Unlike the case of
non-vegetarian food, many plant foods do not even involve
destroying the plant, but only using its produce. It is for
these reasons that a vegetarian diet is more in keeping with
the value of ahimsa and the Vedas consider only plants
and herbs *(aushadhi)* as proper food. (Some also believe
that eating non-vegetarian food physiologically increases
tendencies towards greed, aggression, and selfishness, but I
am not aware of any current research to support this view.)
However, there is no rule which says that the knowledge of
Vedanta is unavailable to a non-vegetarian; being vegetarian can only be considered a very helpful but yet a
peripheral matter.

With this we now conclude our brief look at some
teachings which can be considered peripheral to the heart
of Vedanta.

---

21. This is not to deny the possibility of plants and trees suffering. However,
life depends on consuming another life (even if it is a plant or a fruit or a seed),
and not feeding ourselves to completely avoid injury would result in injury to
our own life. The dictum is not "complete cessation of any injury" but just "least
possible injury."

Are Vedantic Teachings Logical?

One last topic that I would like to deal with, while we are on the subject of the teachings of Vedanta, is the general impression that these teachings are of dubious value because they are not logical or rational but are only mystical. We, in our modern scientific times, take pride in being totally logical and rational, and anything which seems to be beyond the bounds of logic and rationality becomes automatically suspect. This is really unfortunate, because by drawing a small and artificial circle of what we consider acceptable to our intellect, we unnecessarily exclude a vast area of knowledge and truth just because it is outside our own conditioning.

We are very often neither clear about what is actually meant by words like *logical, rational,* and *mystical* nor aware that many of our day-to-day actions, experiences, and conclusions fall outside the ambit of logic and rationality. Let us begin by having the dictionary meanings of these three readily before us:

Logical: Capable of reasoning or using reason in an orderly, cogent fashion.

Rational: Relating to, based on, or agreeable to reason.

Mystical: (a) Having a spiritual meaning or reality that is neither apparent to the senses nor obvious to the intelligence.

             (b) Based on subjective experience (as intuition or insight).

Is Vedanta mystical? Many portions of Vedanta are undoubtedly mystical in terms of the dictionary meaning of that word because these portions deal with matters and concepts which are not apparent to the senses nor obvious to the intelligence. Does this, however, make Vedanta illogical and irrational or, to put the same thing in different words, is Vedanta unreasonable? Here we must guard against the fallacy of automatically assuming that if something does not fall within one viewpoint it must necessarily fall in the camp of a diametrically opposite viewpoint. If something does not fit in our reasoning capacity, it need not always be *against* reason—it could be *beyond* reason.

We are usually justified in testing everything with our faculty of reasoning. Reasoning is an aspect of our intellect which is an important part of our mind. Now, let us look at the subject matter of the portions of Vedanta which we have seen so far. We have talked about the atma, which is the real *us* while the body, the mind, and its intellect are like superimpositions. How can the ultimate subject—I— be made an object of the mind's comprehension? How rational is it to expect to become conscious of consciousness itself or to become aware of awareness itself? Who or what will understand the atma, when the atma is the awareness by which everything else is known and understood? Unlike Descartes' often-quoted statement "I think, therefore I am," which seems to imply that thinking proves our existence, the Vedantic viewpoint is "I am, therefore I think"—that is, we cannot use our thinking ability to be the primary evidence of our existence. The atma is primary and self-evident, whereas the mind is secondary and dependent on the atma; just as a shadow cannot understand the substance, the mind and intellect cannot understand the atma in our usual way of knowing.

But if this is so then what is the role of Vedantic teachings? If one cannot use them by the application of one's mind then how is one to deal with them? The answer here is that Vedanta can work only through our mind and intellect and, therefore, can never make us directly understand the atma as an object of our knowledge or experience—in fact our ability to know or experience anything is because of the atma. All Vedanta can do via our mind is to dispel wrong notions about and false associations with things which we *can* know (such as our body, emotions, and intellect) so that what remains is pure subjectivity in the nature of conscious existence—we can never *know* our real self, we can only *be* our self. Vedanta does talk about matters beyond the mind but it can do so only by making us use our mind and is therefore pitched at that level; because it operates at the level of the mind, a portion of Vedanta is capable of being within our reasoning capacity, but because its objective is to take us beyond the mind, a part of its teachings falls outside the ambit of reasoning.

A useful metaphor here is a lion in our dream which suddenly roars and pounces upon us during our dream stroll in a dream jungle and startles us out of the dream into wakefulness. The lion is part of the dream at the same level as any other object in the dream; however, it is special because it can wake us up into reality without itself gaining any reality. Vedanta is like that dream lion which forms a bridge to a different level of reality without entering that level of reality itself. If this is properly understood, then instead of being stuck on logic and rationality we can go ahead and learn something fundamental and new as long as it does not *offend* our reasoning or *contradict* our valid experiences.

One other factor which gives Vedanta an air of being outside the bounds of reason is the lack of appreciation of the fact that Vedanta is an independent means of knowledge. An independent means of knowledge can have no other proof except proof by its own working. When this is not properly understood, we get involved in frustrating attempts to prove or disprove the teachings of Vedanta without realizing that the means which we use for this purpose happen to be wholly inappropriate in many core areas of Vedanta.

Incidentally, some of our cherished beliefs—such as the earth being flat or the sun revolving around the earth—were based on our sensory perceptions and reasoning ability, but proved to be untrue. Some of the things we treasure the most, like love, have often no logical explanation, but that does not make them unreal. Some of our day-to-day actions, such as smoking or overeating, do not say much about our individual rationality. Some of the values that we collectively pursue in spite of the environmental degradation, the hostility, the oppression, and the final emptiness which they create do not say much about our rationality as a species. Just before the beginning of the twentieth century Max Planck was advised by some very logical and rational scientists not to pursue a career in physics because all problems in physics had already been solved! (Max Planck not only became a physicist but opened up a huge, new, and still mysterious area of quantum mechanics which displaced several hallowed notions of classical physics.) It may also be of interest to note that—according to such philosophical luminaries as Bertrand Russell and Thomas Nagel—if we take logic to its very end, we can never *prove* the existence of anything other than our own selves and our present experiences. Logic and rationality are useful tools which should not be allowed to become blinkers; intuition and insight are valuable even if they cannot be reduced to an algorithm. In the final analysis, the real issue is not whether Vedanta is logical but whether we are logical enough to understand the limits of logic.

To Conclude

We have now completed an initial look at some of the teachings of Vedanta. Our objective has not been to get into a detailed exposition or to go through a comprehensive summary but only to touch upon some fragmented areas in order to get a feel for the nature of these teachings. The contents of this chapter should not be looked upon as adequate material to develop even a preliminary overview of the entire scope of Vedanta; partial knowledge, if not recognized as incomplete, can be much more damaging than no knowledge. In the words of Alexander Pope:

> A little learning is a dang'rous thing;
> Drink deep, or taste not the Pierian spring;
> There shallow draughts intoxicate the brain,
> And drinking largely sobers us again.

Chapter Four

◆

The Texts

THE TEACHINGS OF VEDANTA are contained in the vast treasure-house of Sanskrit literature. The apex of this collection of literature is formed by three texts which are of prime importance. These are the Upanishads, the *Brahma Sutras*, and the *Bhagavad Gita*. However, there are gradations even amongst these three.

The first and foremost texts out of this prime set of texts are, of course, the Upanishads. We have already seen that they are part of the Vedas, which are called *shruti*, meaning *heard* texts. As the Upanishads are not ascribed to any known authors they are looked upon as *revealed* texts, and in keeping with the divine status accorded to them, they are the highest and final authority in respect of all Vedantic teachings. In fact, as far as Vedanta is concerned, the Upanishads are the full-fledged and unique means of knowledge for knowing the true nature of one's own self.

When something is categorized as a primary means of knowledge, this has a number of significant implications. The first implication is that it can have no real substitute.

A further implication is that without this specific means of knowledge it would not be possible to know whatever is to be known by using this particular means. Thus, vision is a specific means of knowledge of colors and it cannot be substituted with another means of knowledge, such as hearing; color cannot be known by somebody who has never had vision. Further, when there is a proper means of knowledge and when all required conditions are fulfilled, then the relevant knowledge must occur, whether we wish it or not—if our eyes are open and not defective, if our mind is not wandering, and if there is enough light falling on an object of large-enough size in front of our eyes then we will have knowledge of the color and form of that object *whether we want that knowledge or not.*

Vedanta not only recognizes five usually known means of knowledge[22]—which we can use for obtaining knowledge of everything other than the atma—but goes on to say that the Upanishads are a sixth unique means of knowledge, for knowledge of the self, which it names *shabda pramana* (words as a means of knowledge). Here the reference is not to words as a means of transference of knowledge already obtained by using some other means of knowledge. Someone can visit a new city and form an impression of it by using their sense organs, or they can come up with a new mathematical formula by using their mental powers. They can then write an article about that city or about their mathematical formula and we can read that article. The words of such an article are *not* shabda pramana. Such words are only a means of communicating something already known by using some other means of knowledge.

On the other hand, the subject of Vedanta—our real self—is something which cannot ever be known by anybody by using the usual means of knowledge, such as

---

22. (i) *pratyaksha* - sense perceptions (ii) *anumana* - inference (iii) *arthapatti* - presumption (iv) *upamana* - correlative knowledge (v) *anuplabdhi* - knowledge of absence.

perception and inference, because the senses and the mind cannot operate on something which itself energizes the senses and the mind. Here the words of the Upanishads (and, of course, further explanation and unfoldment of those words) are the only means of knowledge. As shabda pramana, Vedanta must work without fail every time suitable conditions are fulfilled, and we will examine some of those conditions in the next chapter. On the other hand, the efficacy of Vedanta can never be fully proved or disproved by using our senses or mind but only by actually employing Vedanta in the correct manner ourselves. This is because our senses and mind are not an appropriate means of knowledge for many core areas of Vedanta.

The various ancient Upanishads contain such a variety of different approaches and styles of expression that, at times, their teachings appear confusing and even contradictory, though they all talk about the same great truths. Much later, a well-recognized sage known as Badarayana reduced the essence of the Upanishads to concise and logically arranged aphorisms in a collection known as the *Brahma Sutras*. In terms of hierarchy, these *Brahma Sutras* (also known as the *Vedanta Sutras*) rank in importance next only to the Upanishads. Even though the *Brahma Sutras* are written and organized in a precise and logical fashion, they are still quite difficult to understand and assimilate.

This brings us to the last of the three primary texts: the *Bhagavad Gita*. The *Gita* is a small part of a gigantic work (of 100,000 verses) called the *Mahabharata* authored by the famous sage Vyasa. The *Gita* is much easier to read and understand than the Upanishads and the *Brahma Sutras;* its setting and tone are much more practical and readily applicable to daily life and its problems. It does not get too involved with the more complex reaches of advaita and spends a very significant portion of its contents in laying out preparatory areas like bhakti and proper understanding of actions (karmas) and their results (*karma-phala*). Because of its qualities, its beautiful and powerful poetry, and its emphasis on the concept of a personified god, for a majority of Hindus the *Gita* is the only Vedantic text that they ever get exposed to.

The Upanishads, the *Brahma Sutras*, and the *Bhagavad Gita* are collectively called the *prasthana traya*, "the three starting points" for Vedanta.

A number of learned and well-known teachers have written detailed commentaries on all or some of these three basic texts. Such a commentary, known as a *bhashya*, breaks up the difficult, compounded words of the original text, logically relates different parts of the text, and unfolds the in-depth meanings of words and sentences. Shankara was a prolific *bhashyakar* (commentator), and out of his writings we have available to us even today his bhashyas on ten Upanishads, on the *Brahma Sutras*, and on the *Bhagavad Gita*. The bhashyas of Shankara and several later men of wisdom are invaluable material for understanding the original texts, and so they are very important texts themselves.

Apart from bhashyas, teachers and commentators produced other types of works, such as *karikas* (independent expositions in verse of an original text) and *varttikas* (verses expounding upon a bhashya to bring out what is not said or what is inadequately said in the bhashya). Gaudapada (who is accepted as Shankara's teacher's teacher) is credited with producing the *Mandukya Karika*, which is a large work of 215 verses based on the very short (12 verses) *Mandukya Upanishad* and which contains some of the most sublime advaita thoughts. Sureshvaracharya, a contemporary of Shankara, was a renowned *varttikakar* (writer of varttikas) who wrote, amongst other things, brilliant varttikas on Shankara's bhashyas.

Yet another category of literary works connected with Vedanta is called *tika*, which is the name for a book of explanatory notes on a bhashya or a karika or a varttika along with some additional views.

Bhashyas, karikas, varttikas, and tikas are related directly or indirectly to an original and primary text. There is a whole separate category of writings which revolve around a specific subject or topic as against one original text. Such a work is called a *prakarana*, and is in the nature of a dissertation on a chosen topic (which could be just one facet of Vedanta—or its entire scope). This work can draw upon a number of primary and subsidiary texts related to the chosen topic, apart from the authors' own views. These prakarana works can be very long and detailed (such as the *Vivekachudamani*—attributed with controversy to Shankara—which has 581 verses); others can be concise and yet encapsulate the basic teachings of Vedanta (such as the 53 verses of the *Vakyavritti*, also ascribed to Shankara). Prakarana books exist in large number and grow continuously by works of new authors in every age.

Apart from the traditional listing of categories of Vedantic texts mentioned above, in the last hundred years or so we have had some very useful works which do not fall within these categories. These books are compilations of conversations with and some questions answered by persons of great wisdom, who had full understanding of the deepest teachings of Vedanta but who did not focus on producing elaborate and formal texts. These collections have been put together by students and translators associated with great figures like Ramana Maharshi and Nisargadatta Maharaj. Portions of these works can seem confusing and contradictory because their contents were meant for a specific individual in a specific context; they also depend upon the understanding and interpretation of the editor or translator concerned. In spite of this difficulty, some works of this category contain piercing insights which ring so clearly of timeless truths that they are a joy to read and provide very valuable material for a student of Vedanta.

How does one approach or start with this mass of Vedantic literature? There are no simple answers here. The Upanishads were never meant to be available for study by any curious passerby. They are couched in such language and have such a mystical flavor that for any beginner to just read their bare texts is not only quite meaningless but could also lead to premature and false conclusions or bring about disdain for their contents. Their purpose is not only to instruct but to inspire; their contents are not that of a structured argument but more like a collection of ecstatic snapshots of great truths. Contrary to popular belief, every sentence in the Upanishads is not a statement of the final and absolute truth; there are tentative approaches, interesting debates, stories, and anecdotes, many of which have more to do with questioning and seeking than with answering and finding. It was recognized that their deep and subtle truths were capable of being understood only by those who combined a burning thirst for truth and wisdom along with a high level of intellectual and emotional preparation; there was grave danger of others not only failing to understand their true message but also of drawing wrong under-standing which could be used to support perverse logic and ethical licentiousness.

The best thing of course is to have some selected Upanishads gradually and consistently unfolded to us by an illumined teacher from the basis of personal experience, which is how they were designed to be taught. However, with our general impatience, difficulty in spending much time with a teacher, and the ready availability of scores of books on the Upanishads, it would be unrealistic to suggest that one should read nothing on one's own. If possible, only what is recommended by the teacher should be read; if one must read in an unguided fashion then one can attempt some of the shorter main Upanishads supplemented, in due course, with a commentary of a recognized expert—and here Shankara's name certainly comes to the fore.

Even though the *Brahma Sutras* are very concise and logically arranged, attempts to read them on one's own can be even more frustrating than in the case of the Upanishads—their very brevity and a different style of writing and arguing make the *Brahma Sutras* much more abstruse. As far as I am concerned, I would hesitate to read them even with a commentary, except under the active guidance of a teacher.

The *Bhagavad Gita* lends itself to much easier reading, as it is supposed to; with a commentary it can be an exceptionally valuable text, combining as it does many of the preparatory and core teachings of Vedanta in a work of magnificence and efficacy.

In the supplement to this chapter I have provided translations of some verses from the Upanishads, the *Brahma Sutras*, and the *Bhagavad Gita* with a few of my comments. These are really random selections designed only to provide a flavor of the actual contents of these important texts.

Some prakarana books (for example, the *Vivekachudamani*) and more modern books containing conversations with and answers from truly evolved persons of recent times can be very rewarding reading. Apart from books, we also now have available some audio and video tapes of teachings of some current teachers of Vedanta. The contents and caliber of teaching varies, of course, with the teacher concerned, and even with the best of teachers this is no substitute for live interaction; however, these media provide an interesting supplement to learning from books and I have personally found them to be valuable.

In whatever reading we do, we should bear in mind that there will be many areas of confusion and apparent contradictions even in authoritative texts; some of this can be avoided by recourse to the teacher, and some of it is

unavoidable—it almost seems that the struggle and frustration in trying to arrive at some clear and meaningful vision
is part of the admission price!

While we are on this subject of Vedantic texts and their
classifications, I should mention that instead of literature
pertaining only to Vedanta, if one were to look at the Vedic
religion (or Hinduism) as a whole, then the way of catego-
rizing the available literature is somewhat different from
what we have seen so far. This categorization is only of
peripheral interest to someone beginning to explore
Vedanta; therefore please feel free to skip the remaining
paragraphs of this chapter and go straight to the supplement to this chapter, or even to the beginning of the next
chapter, if you so wish.

The classification of religious texts starts with the four
Vedas *(shruti)* as the primary basis; however, the emphasis
here is not only on the portion containing the Upanishads
(the *jñana kanda*) but also on the much larger earlier
portions (the *karma kanda*). After the four main Vedas
come the four *upa* (subsidiary) Vedas: the *Ayur Veda* (the
science of promoting and extending a healthy life), the
Dhanur Veda (the science of archery and of the use of many
other types of weapons), the *Gandharva Veda* (relating to
music and dance), and the *Artha Shastra* (dealing with
statecraft, politics, and administration, including economic
management).

After these *upa* Vedas, we have the six *Vedangas*, or
explanatory "limbs" of the Vedas. The first two are called
Siksha and *Vyakarana;* they were both written by the sage
Panini and deal with phonetics, pronunciation, and accent,
as well as the precise and detailed grammar for Sanskrit.
Nirukta, the third *Vedanga*, deals with etymology;
Chhandas Shastra, the fourth, teaches prosody and the use
of meters in both prose and poetry. *Kalpa Shastra* and
Jyotisha are the fifth and sixth *Vedangas*, which deal,

respectively, with some detailed rites and rituals, and with astronomy and astrology. Though the *upa* Vedas and *Vedangas* are important and useful, they do not share the exalted status of the four main Vedas.

The next category of Hindu scriptures is called *smriti* (literally, "that which is remembered"). The *smritis* are recognized as human compositions (unlike the Vedas) and cover a very wide range of subjects. An important part of the *smritis* contains rules and regulations governing the conduct of individuals, communities, and the state. There are about eighteen such codes given by different lawmakers of the past, with the best-known being the *Manu Smriti*, the *Yajñavalkya Smriti*, and the *Parashara Smriti*; as such *smritis* deal with ethics and conventions, portions get outdated from time to time.

The *shrutis* and *smritis* were heard, memorized, inter-preted, and implemented by rulers, priests, and scholars. However, the man on the street had neither the ability nor the inclination to get into such erudite texts. His needs were served by two other categories of texts, known as the *itihasas* and the *puranas* (both of which could also be categorized as *smriti* in a broad sense, as they are acknowledged human compositions).

The *itihasas* consist of two great epics, known as the *Ramayana* and the *Mahabharata*; both of these are long and complex tales involving a whole gamut of human behavior and emotions, including love, duty, family rela-tions, righteousness, treachery and war. Values encouraged by dharma are highlighted in a poetic and dramatic way here. These two epics are so famous that there is almost nobody, in even the remotest of villages in India, who does not know their stories or who is not aware of the several values preached by them. These epics, apart from popularizing reli-gious stories and values, also contain some gems of great philosophy as well as codes of conduct in well-known portions such as the *Bhagavad Gita* or the *Shantiparva* (both of which happen to be in the *Mahabharata*).

The *puranas* also contain stories which convey several values and ethics; the stories here are very short and pitched at a level which even children and illiterate adults can understand and enjoy. There are eighteen puranas, which contain stories well-known throughout India, such as those about Bhakta Dhruva, Satyavan and Savitri, Prahlada, Raja Harishchandra, and the like; the better-known puranas are the *Bhagavat*, *Vishnu*, and *Markandeya* puranas. Each purana tends to emphasize a particular deity.

The next set of scriptures, called the *agamas*, lay down doctrines and disciplines for the worship of particular deities. Shaiva, Vaishnava, and Shakta, the three main sects amongst the followers of Hinduism, sprout from the agamas.

The last set of traditional texts deals with the *darshanas* (meaning *visions*), which are really schools of philosophy, meant for intellectually well-endowed persons and for scholars. As we saw in the first chapter, tradition lists six such *astika* schools (those which recognize the final authority of the Vedas), including Vedanta. Teachers and proponents of each school have produced various texts of different levels of complexity to meet the needs of diverse types of people included amongst their followers.

As students of Vedanta our concern would be more with purely Vedantic texts. However, I have included this brief outline of religious texts and their categories because some background knowledge of the Hindu religion is certainly helpful; later, the understanding of other philosophical lines of thinking is important for firmly establishing that Vedanta is not merely one of the several schools of philosophy but contains unique and unchallengeable truths along with an unparalleled teaching methodology.

Supplement

◆

Selections of translated extracts from the Upanishads, the *Brahma Sutras*, and the *Bhagavad Gita*

The Upanishads

Before we look at some sample material from a few Upanishads, I would like to show how some deceptively simple-sounding lines from the Upanishads can result in a large number of greatly varying translations and lead to both confusion and controversy. For this purpose I am going to use and paraphrase (with the author's permission) some of the work contained in the first chapter of Ananda Wood's interesting book called *Interpreting the Upanishads*. The example used here is the rather well-known four-line peace invocation from the *Isha Upanishad*[23] which, in Sanskrit, reads:

> purnam adah purnam idam
> purnat purnam udachyate
> purnasya purnam adaya
> purnam eva 'vashishyate.

---

23. The *Isha Upanishad* is traditionally the first Upanishad to be taken up for study out of the ten so-called principal Upanishads. This peace invocation is placed at the very beginning of the *Isha Upanishad* and is, therefore, likely to be the first thing to be read when anyone commences a study of the actual texts of the Upanishads. Incidentally, the same invocation is also found in the *Brihadaranyaka Upanishad*.

Literally translated into English, this passage would read:

The full, that; the full, this.
From the full, the full arises.
Of the full, the full taken back,
the full alone remains.

Such a translation sounds very awkward; also, after reading this sort of thing, one could be justified in concluding that if such material is representative of the profound and sublime substance of the Upanishads, one may as well not waste much time over them because their contents appear to be banal or ridiculous or both!

Better translations would, of course, improve readability and may sound a little more meaningful. Let us look at a few examples of different translations of the same passage:

(i)   That is full; this is full.
      The full comes out of the full.
      Taking the full from the full,
      the full itself remains.
         (Dr. S. Radhakrishnan—*The Principal Upanishads*)

(ii) Fullness beyond, fullness here:
      Fullness from fullness doth proceed.
      From fullness, fullness take away:
      Fullness yet remains.
                  (R. C. Zaehner—*Hindu Scriptures*)

(iii) That is perfect. This is perfect.
      Perfect comes from perfect.
      Take perfect from perfect,
      the remainder is perfect.
                  (Purohit Swami & W. B. Yeats—
                  The Ten Principal Upanishads)

(iv) The invisible is the Infinite, the visible too is the
      Infinite.
      From the Infinite, the visible universe of infinite
      expansion has come out.
      The Infinite remains the same, even though the
      infinite universe has come out of it.
                    (Swami Sarvananda—*Isavasyopanisad*)

Finally, a retelling (not a simple translation) of the same
verses from Ananda Wood's *From the Upanishads*:

(v)   That self out there, this self in here,
      each is reality, complete:
      from which arises everything,
      to which all things return again,
      in which all seeming things consist;
      which stays the same, unchanged, complete.

There are several more ways of translating and para-
phrasing this same small passage. What do these differing
interpretations show? They show, at least, that one short
set of verses in simple language can throw up and bring
into question several fundamental concepts like *fullness*,
perfection, *infinite*, and *reality*. Further, all these translations and interpretations, however accurate, well-meant,
and insightful, will not go very far on their own to bring
out the true, deep, and beautiful meaning which this
passage really contains.

The point here is not to try to understand the full and
proper meaning of this particular set of verses but just to
see the general difficulty in extracting real meaning from
such cryptic and mystical writing.

Having said this, we will now look at translations of
a few selected passages from three different Upanishads.
These passages have been selected so that they are a little

easier to understand than the example we have just seen; they also have some connection with a few of the concepts which we have already gone over in chapter 3. The translations are from Swami Sivananda's *The Principal Upanishads*.

(a) From the *Mundaka Upanishad* (of the *Atharva Veda*):
Shaunaka, the great householder, approached Angiras in the manner laid down by the scriptures and asked: "What is that, O Lord, which being known, all this becomes known?"

To him, Angiras replied: "There are two kinds of knowledge to be acquired, so say those who know, namely *para* [the higher] and *apara* [the lower]. Of these the *apara* [lower knowledge] is the *Rig Veda*, the *Sama Veda*, the *Yajur Veda*, the *Atharva Veda* [the four Vedas], *siksha*, *kalpa*, *vyakarna*, *nirukta*, *chhandas*, and *jyotisha* [knowledge dealing with phonetics, rituals, grammar, etymology, meter, and astrology]. But *para* [higher knowledge] is that by which the imperishable is known. (I.1.3–5)

[Continuation of the words of Angiras:] Let an aspirant [or student], after he has examined the worlds gained by karma, acquire freedom from all desires, reflecting that the eternal cannot be gained by karma. Let him, in order to obtain the knowledge of the eternal, take sacrificial fuel in his hands and approach that teacher alone who is well-versed in the Vedas and is established in [committed to] brahman.

To that pupil who has approached him respectfully, whose mind is at rest and whose senses are subdued, let the wise teacher teach that *brahma vidya* [knowledge of brahman] through which the true, immortal *purusha* is known." (I.2.12–13)

(b) From the *Kena Upanishad* (of the *Sama Veda*):

[Student:] Who impels the mind to alight on objects? At whose command does prana [vital breath or life-force] proceed to function? At whose command do men utter speech? What intelligence directs the eyes and ears?

[Teacher:] It is the ear of the ear, the mind of the mind, the tongue of the tongue, and also life of the life and eye of the eye. Having abandoned [the sense of *I*-ness in these] and rising above sense-life, the wise become immortal. The eye does not go there, nor speech, nor the mind. We do not therefore know how to instruct one about it. It is different from what is known and it is beyond what is unknown. Thus we have heard from the ancient sages who taught us that. What speech does not enlighten but what enlightens speech, know that alone as brahman and not this which people here worship. What one cannot think with the mind but by which they say that the mind is made to think, know that alone as brahman and not this which people here worship.[24] (1.1–5)

[Teacher:] It is known by him who thinks he knows not; he who thinks he knows, does not know. It is unknown to those who know and known to those who do not know. Brahman is known well when it is known as the witness of every state of consciousness; by such knowledge is attained immortality. (2.3–4)

(c) From the *Katha Upanishad* (of the *Yajur Veda*):

A part of this beautiful Upanishad is in the form of a conversation between Nachiketas and Yama. Nachiketas is a young but wise and dutiful prince who goes to meet

24. The phrase "and not this which people here worship" refers to gods and deities worshipped by people, but should not be taken to mean a blanket condemnation of all worship.

Yama, the god of death. Yama, pleased with the behavior and wisdom of Nachiketas, grants him three boons. What Nachiketas asks for and gets as his first two boons is philosophically less important, so we will start with the part where Nachiketas asks Yama for his third boon.

[Nachiketas:] There is that doubt that when a man is dead, some say he is and some say he is not. This I would like to know, taught by you. This is the third of my boons.

[Yama:] On this point even the gods of olden times had doubts. It is not easy to understand this—subtle is its nature. Nachiketas, choose another boon; do not press me on this; give this up for me.

[Nachiketas:] You say, O death, that even the gods had doubts here and that this is not easy to know. Another teacher like you is not to be found; surely, there is no other boon like this.

[Yama:] Choose sons and grandsons who may live a hundred years, herds of cattle and elephants, gold and horses. Choose the wide abode of the earth and live yourself as many years as you like. If you can think of any [other] boon equal to that [wealth and long life], ask for it. Be a king of the wide earth. I will make you the enjoyer of all desires. Whatever desires are difficult to attain in the world of mortals, ask for them according to your wish. Fair maidens with their chariots and musical instruments not available for enjoyment by mortals—be attended upon by them, I will give them to you. But, O Nachiketas, do not ask the question of the state of the soul after death.

[Nachiketas:] These things last only till tomorrow. O death, they wear out the vigor of all the senses. Even the longest life is really short. Please keep your chariots, dance, and music. No man can be made happy by wealth. If we [mortals] should obtain wealth and behold you [the god of death], we would live only as long as you ordain. Only that boon which I have chosen is fit to be longed for by me. (I.1.20–27)

[Yama:] The good *[shreya]* and the pleasant *[preya]* take hold of all men. The wise man examines and distinguishes them. The wise man prefers the good to the pleasant but the ignorant man chooses the pleasant for the sake of the body. O Nachiketas, you have renounced objects of desire and of pleasant shape, judging them by their real value. You have not chosen the road of wealth on which many men perish. The two paths of ignorance and knowledge are wide apart and lead to different goals. You, Nachiketas, desire knowledge, for even many desires have not shaken you. The ignorant, who live in the midst of darkness but fancy themselves as wise and learned, go round and round deluded in many ways, just as blind people led by the blind. The way to the hereafter is not apparent to the ignorant man who is foolish, deluded by wealth. "This is the world," he thinks, "there is no other." Thus, he falls again and again under my sway. He [the self or the atma] is of whom many are not even able to hear; whom many, even when they hear of him, do not comprehend. Wonderful is the man who, when found, is able to teach [about] the self; wonderful is he [the student] who comprehends the self, when taught by an able teacher. That self, when taught by a man of inferior intellect, is not easy to be known, as it is to be thought of in various ways. But when it is taught by a knower who is one with brahman, there are no doubts concerning it. The self is subtler than the subtle and is not to be obtained by arguing. (I.2.2–8)

[Yama:] The intelligent atma is not born nor does he die; he did not spring [was not born] from anything and nothing sprang from him; unborn, eternal, everlasting, ancient, he is not slain though the body is slain. If the slayer thinks "I slay," if the slain thinks "I am slain," then both of them do not know well. This [the atma] slays not, nor is slain. The atma, subtler than the subtle, greater than the great, is seated in the heart of each living being. He [the individual human being] who is free from desire, with his mind and senses composed, beholds the majesty of the self and becomes free from sorrow. . . . The wise man, who knows the atma as bodiless, seated firmly in perishable bodies, great and all-pervading, never grieves. This atma cannot be obtained by study of the Vedas, nor by intelligence, nor by much hearing. He whom the self chooses, by him the self can be gained. To him this atma reveals its true nature.

But he who has not turned away from bad conduct, whose senses are not subdued, whose mind is not concentrated, whose mind is not pacified, can never obtain this atma by knowledge. (I.2.18–20,22–24)

[Yama:] Arise, awake, having reached the great [teachers], learn [realize the atma]. Like the sharp edge of a razor is that path, difficult to cross and hard to tread—thus the wise say. (I.3.14)

[Yama:] The ignorant run after external objects of desire and fall into the snare of widespread death, but wise men, knowing the nature of immortality, do not covet the fleeting things here. To the self by which one knows form, taste, smell, sound, touch, and sensual gratification, nothing remains unknown. This [self] is verily that [brahman]. The wise man, when he knows that by which he perceives all objects in dream or in waking is the great omnipresent atma, grieves no more. (I.1.2–4)

[Yama:] When this atma who dwells in the body departs from the body, what remains then? This verily is that.

Not by *prana* nor by *apana*[25] does any mortal live but it is by some other, on which these two depend, that men live. . . . Some *jivas* [souls] enter the womb in order to have a body, others go into inorganic matter according to their karma and knowledge. . . . As the one fire, after it has entered the world, though one, takes different forms according to whatever it burns, so does the internal atma of all living beings, though one, take a form according to whatever he enters and is outside all forms. . . . As the sun, the eye of the whole world, is not contaminated by the defects of the eye or of external things, so the one internal atma of all living beings is not contaminated by the misery of the world, being external to it. . . . The wise who behold the self as the eternal among the transient, as conscious among the unconscious, who, though one, grants the desires of many, as dwelling in their own selves, to them belongs eternal peace, not to others. They [the sages] perceive that indescribable highest bliss as "This is That." How shall I know that?

Does it shine [of itself] or does it shine by another light? . . . The sun does not shine there, nor do the moon and stars; neither does lightning, and much less this fire [i.e., of man's making or understanding]. When he shines, everything shines after him; by this light everything here shines. (I.2.4,5,7,9,11,13–15)

---

25. *Prana* and *apana* are names of the first two of a list of five different vital breaths or life-forces (collectively also called *prana*) in a living body.

[Yama:] If here [in this life] one is able to comprehend him before the death of the body, he will be liberated from the bondage of the world; if one is not able to comprehend him, then he has to take a body again in the worlds of creation. . . . His form is not to be seen. No one beholds him with the eye. By controlling the mind by the intellect and by incessant meditation he is revealed. Those who know this [brahman] become immortal. . . . The self cannot be reached by speech, by mind, or by the eye. How can it be realized otherwise than from those who say "He is"? (II.2.4,9,12)

We will now here end our look at some material from the Upanishads and turn to the *Brahma Sutras*.

The Brahma Sutras

We have already noted that the *Brahma Sutras* are concise and logically arranged aphorisms containing the essence of the knowledge spread over the various Upanishads. There are 555 individual sutras. Let us start at the very beginning and see the first few, from Swami Vireswarananda's translation and commentary based on Shankara's bhashya.

(i)   *athato brahmajijñasa* (1.1.1)
      Now therefore the inquiry into brahman

Though this certainly is a rather good example of conciseness, it does not seem to convey any significant meaning! As the first step, more implied meaning has to be read into each word, using complex but established rules of Sanskrit grammar, logic, and interpretation. So, a sort of expanded translation of this sutra would be:

<u>Now</u> (after the attainment of the requisite preparatory spiritual and other qualities) <u>therefore</u> (because the results obtained by karmas—including Vedic sacrifices and so on—are ephemeral, whereas the result of the knowledge of brahman is eternal) <u>the inquiry into</u> (the real nature of) <u>brahman</u> (which is beset with doubts owing to the conflicting views of various schools of philosophy).

After this, we can go further into the detailed commentary of a master like Shankara to get full meaning based on proper arguments and interpretation. We will obviously not get into that level of examination here; we will only look at the literal translation, followed by a slightly more expanded meaning, of just three more sutras.

(ii) *janmadhyas yatah* (1.1.2)
    From which the origin, etc. of this

    (Brahman is that omniscient, omnipotent cause) <u>from which</u> (proceed) <u>the origin, etc.</u> (i.e., sustenance and dissolution) <u>of this</u> (world).

(iii) *shastryonitvat* (1.1.3)
    The scriptures being the means of right knowledge

    <u>The scriptures</u> (alone) <u>being the means of right knowledge</u> (with regard to brahman). [This also corroborates and clarifies the previous sutra so that brahman as the cause of this world is established by scriptural authority and not only by inference, etc.]

(iv) *tat tu samanvyat* (1.1.4)
That but because it is the main purport

> But that (brahman is to be known only from the
> scriptures and not independently by any other
> means is established) because it is the main
> purport (of all Vedanta texts).[26]

There is not much point in reproducing translations of
more sutras, not only because the arguments get quite
involved but also because they presuppose familiarity with
the Upanishads. We will, therefore, now proceed to look at
some material from the *Bhagavad Gita*.

The Bhagavad Gita

The *Bhagavad Gita* literally means "The Song of the
Lord" and is not to be confused with the *Bhagavat*,
which is used to refer to the completely different *Bhagavat
purana*. As said earlier, the *Bhagavad Gita* is a small part
of a grand epic, called the *Mahabharata*, written by the
famous sage Vyasa. The *Mahabharata* is a long and compli-
cated tale connected with the ruling family of the ancient
Indian kingdom of Hastinapur. Over a long time and after
many events, a stage is reached when the differences
between two sets of cousins from this ruling family can be
settled only by war. The two sets of cousins are called the
Pandavas (who represent righteousness) and the Kauravas
(who have a track record of injustice, aggression, and
betrayal, fueled by greed and jealousy).

Arjuna is the name of one of the Pandava brothers and

---

26. You may have picked up the apparent contradiction between this sutra
(which says that brahman is to be known only from the scriptures) and the
portion of the *Katha Upanishad* given earlier which says that the atma cannot be
obtained by the study of the Vedas. If you have noticed this problem, please do
not be concerned. Vedanta is replete with such seeming confusion but it all does
get clarified and ultimately comes together quite sensibly.

he is an ace archer whose performance in battle is likely to be the decisive factor in the whole war. Arjuna's charioteer is Krishna, who is portrayed as a divine being incarnated in a human form to deal with the decline of righteousness. Just before the formal war begins, Arjuna asks Krishna to drive his chariot to the neutral space between the two armies arrayed against each other, so that he can take stock of the enemy's resources. The enemy obviously consists of Arjuna's own cousins (the Kauravas) as well as many other relations, patriarchs, and teachers who, for a variety of reasons, feel compelled to side with the Kauravas even though their cause is unjust. Upon being face to face with the fact that the people he will have to fight and kill in battle include his close relations, respected elders, and teachers, Arjuna is overcome with emotion; he comes to the conclusion that rather than enter into this heinous war, he will give up his rightful claims against the Kauravas and become a wandering mendicant, living on alms and disengaged from usual life. At this stage, Krishna exhorts him to do battle for a cause which is just and in keeping with Arjuna's duties as a ruling-class warrior. It is this dialogue between Arjuna and Krishna which is the *Bhagavad Gita* and which contains sublime wisdom set out in beautiful poetry. Arjuna, of course, is representative of each one of us who is not able to sensibly deal with conflicting emotions and desires due to lack of knowledge of our own true self. Krishna, though he appears as a personified god on earth, is really the atma underlying each one of us.

With this background in mind we can now look at some selected verses from the *Bhagavad Gita*. The chosen verses as given below are not all in the actual sequence in which they appear in the *Bhagavad Gita*; some have been rearranged and regrouped to bring together material dealing with a single topic. The translation is from Swami Chidbhavananda's

work on the *Bhagavad Gita*, published by Sri Ramakrishna
Tapovanam, Trichy, India.

We start with verses from the second chapter of the *Gita*,
in which Krishna begins his teachings by telling Arjuna
something about the atma:

> You grieve for those who should not be grieved for;
> yet you spell words of wisdom. The wise grieve
> neither for the living nor for the dead. (2.11)

> The unreal has no existence; the real never ceases to be.
> The truth about both has been realized by the seers.

> Know that to be verily indestructible by which all this
> is pervaded. None can effect the destruction of the
> immutable.

> These bodies of the indweller, who is eternal, inde-
> structible and immeasurable, are said to have an end.
> Fight therefore, O Bharata [Arjuna].

> He who holds atma as slayer and he who considers It
> as the slain, both of them are ignorant. It slays not,
> nor is It slain.

> The atma is neither born nor does It die. Coming into
> being and ceasing to be do not take place in It. Un-
> born, eternal, constant, and ancient, It is not killed
> when the body is slain. (2.16–20)

On a different plane and just to bring about initial settlement of Arjuna's mind, Krishna advances some other arguments to deal with his emotions:

> If you conceive of atma as given to constant births and
> deaths, even then, O mighty-armed [Arjuna], you
> should not sorrow.

Death is certain of that which is born; birth is certain of that which is dead. You should not therefore lament over the inevitable.

Beings are all, O Bharata [Arjuna], unmanifested in their origin, manifested in their mid-state, and unmanifested again in their end. What is the point then for anguish? (2.26–28)

We will now look at some verses from chapter 13 of the *Gita*, which bring out the fact that the knower *(kshetrajña)* is always different from the entire field of what is known *(kshetra)* and that the only real wisdom is the knowledge of the known as well as of the knower:

This body, O Kaunteya [Arjuna], is called kshetra, the field; he who knows it is called kshetrajña by the sages.

And know me as the kshetrajña in all kshetras, O Bharata [Arjuna]. The knowledge of kshetra and kshetrajña is deemed by me as true knowledge.

Hear briefly from me, what the kshetra is, what its properties are, what its modifications are, whence is what; and who he is and what his powers are.

This has been sung by rishis in many ways, in various distinctive chants, in passages indicative of brahman, full of reasoning and convincing.

The great elements, egoism, intellect, as also the unmanifested, the ten senses and the one mind, and the five objects of the senses;

Desire, hatred, pleasure, pain, the aggregate, intelligence, firmness—the kshetra has been thus briefly described with its modifications.

Humility, modesty, non-injury, forbearance, upright-
ness, service of the teacher, purity, steadfastness, self-
control;

Dispassion towards the objects of the senses, and also
absence of egoism, perception of evil in birth, death,
old age, sickness, and pain;

Unattachment, non-identification of self with son,
wife, home, and the like, and constant equanimity in
the occurrence of the desirable and the undesirable;

Unswerving devotion to me in yoga of non-separation,
resort to sequestered places, distaste for the society of
men;

Constancy in self-knowledge, perception of the end
[objective] of the knowledge of truth; this is declared
to be knowledge, and what is opposed to it is ignorance.

I shall describe that which has to be known, knowing
which one attains to immortality. Beginningless is the
supreme brahman. It is not said to be *sat* or *asat*.

With hands and feet everywhere, with eyes and heads
and mouths everywhere, with ears everywhere—he
exists enveloping all.

Shining by the functions of all the senses, yet without
the senses; Absolute, yet sustaining all; devoid of
gunas,[27] yet, he experiences them.

Without and within all beings; the unmoving and also
the moving; because of his subtlety he is incomprehensible; he is far and near.

27. The entire manifestation, including tendencies of individual human beings, is said to
be based on combinations of three basic forces, called *gunas;* these are *sattva* (characterized
by purity, knowledge, and light), *rajas* (characterized by energy, activity, and ambition),
and *tamas* (characterized by ignorance, darkness, and inertia).

He is undivided and yet he seems to be divided in beings. He is to be known as the supporter of beings. He devours and he generates.

The light of all lights, he is said to be beyond darkness; knowledge, the knowable, the goal of knowledge, seated in the hearts of all.

Thus the kshetra, knowledge, and that which has to be known have been briefly described. My devotee, on knowing this, is fitted for my state. (13.1–18)

At various places in the *Gita* Krishna makes it clear to Arjuna that running away from action and life is never an answer; true happiness can come only from using skill and discrimination in choosing appropriate action and then maintaining equanimity irrespective of the actual results. This balance has to be based on the understanding that while action is up to an individual, its results are affected by numerous factors beyond the individual:

Man gains not actionlessness by abstaining from activity, nor does he rise to perfection by mere renunciation. (3.4)

Engage yourself in obligatory work; for action is superior to inaction, and if inactive, even the mere maintenance of your body would not be possible. (3.8)

Seek to perform your duty; but lay not claim to its fruits. Be you not the producer of the fruits of karma; neither shall you lean towards inaction.

Perform action, O Dhananjaya [Arjuna], being fixed in yoga, renouncing attachments, and even-minded in success and failure; equilibrium is verily yoga.

Motivated karma is, O Dhananjaya [Arjuna], far

inferior to that performed in the equanimity of mind; take refuge in the evenness of the mind; wretched are the result-seekers.

The one fixed in equanimity of mind frees oneself in this life from vice and virtue alike; therefore devote yourself to yoga; work done to perfection is verily yoga.[28]

The wise, imbued with evenness of mind, renouncing the fruits of their actions, freed from the fetters of births, verily go to the stainless state. (2.47–51)

We will now look at some verses talking about different types of seekers and the ultimate futility of Vedic rituals for those whose goal is not the finite and the temporal but only the unchanging and eternal:

Four types of virtuous men worship me, O Arjuna: the man in distress, the man seeking knowledge, the man seeking wealth, and the man imbued with wisdom, O the best of the Bharatas [Arjuna]. (7.16)

Of these, the wise man, ever steadfast and devoted to the One, excels; for, supremely dear am I to the wise and he is dear to me. (7.17)

But the fruit that accrues to those men of small intellect is finite. The worshippers of the gods go to the gods; my devotees come to me. (7.23)

Men of poor understanding think of me, the unmanifest, as having manifestation, not knowing my supreme state—immutable and unsurpassed. (7.24)

The unwise who delight in the flowery words

---

28. "Yoga is skill in applying understanding to work" is a more meaningful translation here.

disputing about the Vedas say that there is nothing other than this.

Who are desire-ridden, who hold the attainment of heaven as the goal of birth and its activities, whose words are laden with specific rites bringing in pleasure and lordship.

There is no fixity of mind for them who cling to pleasure and power and whose discrimination is stolen away.

The Vedas enumerate the three gunas. You transcend the three gunas, O Arjuna. Be free from the pairs of opposites, ever-balanced, unconcerned with getting and keeping, and centered in the self.

To an enlightened brahmana all the Vedas are as useful as a tank when there is a flood everywhere. (2.42–46)

Like several other chapters, chapter 14 of the *Gita* contains some descriptions of a person who has firm and settled self-knowledge:

He, O Pandava [Arjuna], who hates not light, activity, and delusion, when present, nor longs after them when absent;

He who, sitting like one unconcerned, is moved not by the gunas, who, knowing that the gunas operate, is firm and moves not;

Balanced in pleasure and pain, self-abiding, viewing a clod of earth, a stone, and gold alike; the same to agreeable and disagreeable, firm, the same in censure and praise;

The same in honor and dishonor, the same to friend and foe, abandoning all undertakings—he is said to have risen above the gunas.

And he who serves me with an unswerving devotion, he, going beyond the gunas, is fitted for becoming brahman.

For I am the abode of brahman, the immortal, and the immutable, the eternal dharma and absolute bliss. (14.22–27)

We end by looking at two different verses from chapter 18, which is the last chapter of the *Gita*. The first verse is an injunction to Arjuna about indiscriminate dissemination of self-knowledge to the unqualified:

This is never to be spoken by you to one who is devoid of austerities, nor to one who is not devoted, nor to one who does not do service, nor to one who speaks ill of me. (18.67)

The other verse brings out the important fact that no matter who the teacher and no matter how good the teaching, ultimately it is the student who has to understand and then base their actions upon their own understanding:

Thus has wisdom more profound than all profundities been declared to you by me. Reflect upon it fully and act as you choose. (18.63)

Chapter Five

◆

About Students, Teachers, and Learning

The Student

Anybody who applies their mental faculties to the acquisition of knowledge in a particular field can be called a student. The Sanskrit word for student is *vidyarthi*, which means a person whose objective is to obtain knowledge. However, when we speak of a student of Vedanta we do not include someone who wishes to know the contents of the Upanishads and other Vedanta texts as scholarly knowledge or as information to satisfy curiosity. A student of Vedanta is not just a vidyarthi or any seeker of knowledge; they have to be, first and foremost, a seeker of moksha, of liberation.

This means that a proper student of Vedanta should have already realized the futility of the usual means and efforts in finding lasting fulfillment. Based on discrimination and analysis of their personal experiences, such a student should have come to the conclusion that no amount of possessions, changes, and achievements can ever satisfy the perennial sense of lacking and wanting; they should then have decided to tackle the problem at its root by going into the nature and validity of the very sense of lacking and wanting. This seeking of liberation from the sense of limitation in general, as against only trying to cope with each individual want, is what converts a person into a *mumukshu* (which is the Sanskrit word for the seeker of moksha).

But this is not all. There is one more step to be taken before a person becomes a proper student of Vedanta. A mumukshu is convinced that their salvation lies in tackling the fundamental sense of being a wanting person. However, they need not have come to any conclusion about *how* to go about doing this, or they may have decided to rely on methods such as trying to quash desires and emotions in order to be liberated. This is not the way of Vedanta, which says that understanding the true nature of the self, by the removal of ignorance surrounding it, is the only solution. A mumukshu who is convinced of this then becomes a seeker of knowledge alone for solving the fundamental human problem and is termed a *jijñasu* in Sanskrit; it is such a seeker of self-knowledge who is the real student of Vedanta.

This student needs certain personal qualities and an adequate amount of preparatory work if they are to draw proper understanding from Vedanta's core teachings. Only such a qualified person is eligible to enter the inner portals of Vedanta. The Sanskrit word for *eligibility* or *entitlement* is *adhikaritvam*, and an eligible person is called an *adhikari*. It is important to understand what makes a person an adhikari; if adhikaritvam is not understood and is not obtained in adequate amount then no amount of mere study will bring proper results. On the other hand, attempts to become an adhikari should not become some misguided battle towards absolute control over all physical and emotional needs or frantic efforts towards total ethical perfection. We will return to this point later, but first let us look at the traditional list of four attributes which make a person into an adhikari, eligible for employing Vedanta as a means of self-knowledge. This list is called *sadhana chatushtaya (four means)* and is to be found, among other places, in the *Vivekachudamani,* which is, as mentioned earlier, a beautiful prakarana-type text usually attributed to Shankara.

Let us look at verse 17 of the *Vivekachudamani,* which reads:

vivekino viraktasya shamadigunashalin mumuk-shorevhi brahmajijñasayogyata matah.

He alone is considered qualified to enquire into the absolute reality who has discrimination, detachment, a collection of certain qualities beginning with a settled mind, and a burning desire for liberation.

Thus, the traditional four qualifications or attributes to be possessed by a fit student are:

1. *viveka,* or discrimination.
2. *vairagya,* or detachment.
3. *shamadiguna,* or a collection of certain qualities beginning with a settled mind (this collection, as we will shortly see, consists of a sub-list of six different qualities).
4. *mumukshutvam,* or a seeking for fundamental libera-tion.

We can now briefly look at each of these qualifications.

1. *Viveka,* or discrimination, is amplified in the texts to be *nityanitya vastu viveka,* or proper understanding of the eternal and the time-bound. However, this is just a way of expression and it cannot literally mean what it apparently says. If we had full and proper understanding of the

eternal[29] at the *beginning* of our Vedantic study, then we would not *need* to do any study, because we would already be knowledgeable, or *jñanis!* At the initial stage, viveka really means that by using our own experience and thinking, we should have come to the conclusion that all that we know and all that we have worked for or achieved is *anitya*, or time-bound. On the other hand, at this stage, we can understand *nitya* or eternal only as a concept which is negatively taken to mean the opposite of time-bound but which is now to be properly and positively understood by study of the texts as unfolded by the teacher.

2. *Vairagya*, or detachment, is explained as *ihamu-traphalabhoga vairagya*, or lack of desire to enjoy the fruits of actions, either here or in the hereinafter. Thus, even a charitable or a religious act with the desire to enjoy the resulting *punya* (good results), leading to a comfortable life now or later or even a place in heaven, would not be in keeping with this explanation of vairagya. We must be careful here not to look at detachment as being synonymous with physical renunciation or outward asceticism. Detachment follows discrimination, whereby we stop imposing a false extra value to an object or to a situation which does not actually belong to it. Let us take the instance of money. Detachment does not mean that we should work on convincing ourselves that money has no value. Money, of course, has value in many areas of life and should be used as appropriate. However, objectivity is lost and superimposition of false, subjective values takes place when we look upon money as the real means of dealing with our sense of insecurity. Money, by its very nature, cannot provide a permanent solution to our insecurities if our own nature is insecure; our personal experiences would tell us this if we analyzed them with discrimination. Detachment from

---

29. "Eternal" is a word we all use without real understanding, because we actually do not know or have experience of anything truly eternal.

falsely superimposed values, properly understood after employing discrimination, is what is meant by vairagya.

3. The next item on the list is a collection of six qualities, beginning with *shama*. Let us take a look at each of these six items:

3a. *Shama* is a description of a settled or a resolved state of mind, coming out of a certain acceptance of one's own body and mind as well as by properly managing one's likes and dislikes. A very important factor here is the understanding of God as being the natural order which makes the world as it is and which makes all people (including the student of Vedanta) what they are. This, in turn, makes us accept the inevitable unpleasant situations (and unpleasant persons) neither out of resignation nor out of tolerance but out of seeing the common and orderly creator behind everything and everybody. With shama, our mind is available to us and is under our control, in our pursuit of Vedanta, instead of it being controlled by situations, people, and likes and dislikes.

3b. *Dama* means restraint or control and actually precedes shama in practice. While shama is a product of maturity, dama is will-based regulation of the senses (and of reactions) to stay away from situations and to control impulses which need to be avoided till shama develops. In a situation capable of provoking anger, the absence of anger would be shama but the restraint of one's speech or hand, once anger has arisen, would be dama. One can see that once maturity is achieved, the importance of dama is not so great, in the sense that an occasion for the use of dama will not arise if shama is already present.

3c. *Uparati* has connotations of love or enjoyment. We, as students, may be intellectually clear about the value of our pursuit but, yet, may be emotionally distant. By spiritual practice and by association with other spiritual seekers we develop a love for spirituality so that other pursuits automatically lose their hold, the mind does not lean on external objects for its joy and, consequently, the usually strong sense of *me* and *mine* begins to dissipate.

3d. *Titiksha* is the capacity to endure. It is the capacity to put up with unpleasant situations and people, patiently and with equanimity. Further, such putting up has to be without lament, complaint, or seeking revenge, and also without great effort to change things. This can come only from objectivity (based on the understanding that all lives must face pairs of opposites like success and failure or pleasant and unpleasant) and from the conviction that the only goal worth pursuing is the goal of knowledge of the self.

3e. *Shraddha* is often translated as *faith* but it is not really just faith in the sense of blind belief; if this were so then Vedanta would be dogma to be preached and not knowledge to be understood. However, when Vedanta says "You are the whole" this is not something to be believed but something to be understood. Shraddha here only implies trust in the words of the teacher and of the scriptures pending discovery of the truth by the student. What is required is the ability to give the teachings and the teacher the benefit of any doubt and the suspension of prejudice, cynicism, and skepticism until and unless what is being taught irreconcilably contradicts our valid experiences or outrages our other means of knowledge. In a sense, shraddha is the initial acceptance of the Upanishads as a completely independent means of knowledge which can be proven only after its own and proper use. This is difficult, but without shraddha there is no real way of going forward.

3f. *Samadhana* is the ability to concentrate upon a given subject for an appropriate length of time. To understand and assimilate the teachings of Vedanta requires a mind which can hold experiences and complex ideas, dwell upon them, and be absorbed in the study and understanding of a particular topic. This ability requires a certain amount of intellectual development and practice as well as emotional tranquility.

4. We now come to the fourth and last item on our main list, which is *mumukshutvam*, or a burning desire for liberation. We have already talked about a mumukshu as being a spiritual seeker who wants to fundamentally tackle the human being's perennial sense of lacking and wanting. For an eligible student of Vedanta, moksha should not be one of many desires, but the predominant desire. The desire for liberation may start as a simple, manageable, and deferrable desire (like initial thirst) but, in time, has to become all-consuming like a burning thirst. This does not mean that the student of Vedanta should have no other desires at all, but it does mean that those other desires should, in time, become subservient to the paramount desire for ultimate and permanent freedom.

Incidentally, while mumukshutvam happens to be the last item in the list of qualifications, it is probably the most critical. Someone who has never been consumed by a longing for the ultimate answer is not likely to penetrate to the heart of Vedanta. How is the desire to have self-knowledge different from any other desire? Why is learning Vedanta not just another becoming—from a person who does not know Vedanta to a person who has understood Vedanta? The answer is that while other desires and efforts deal with a specific want, Vedanta dispels the notion of being limited at the most fundamental level of our existence. Of course, the pursuit of Vedanta does start like any other usual pursuit, as an attempt at another becoming, an attempt to achieve something, an attempt to fill a perceived void. However, Vedanta questions this perception and can lead to the destruction of the very reason for turning to Vedanta: a sense of limitation and bondage. Other pursuits do not tackle the problem at its fundamental level and, therefore, they only perpetuate the basic problem.

We said earlier that without all the qualities which we

have just reviewed there would be no adhikaritvam, no eligibility, and that without some minimum eligibility the teachings of Vedanta will not work at all—not being an adhikari makes the pursuit of Vedanta not merely difficult but almost meaningless. On the other hand, we also said that being an adhikari does not mean some impossible attempt at total objectivity and control or at full understanding and ethical purity. A person with full measure of adhikaritvam is not a mumukshu or a jijñasu but a man of total wisdom! A person who is a full *viveki*—that is, who totally understands what is eternal—does not need to study Vedanta. Similarly, uparati does not mean that a student should completely lose a sense of *me* and *mine* as a precondition; all that is required at the initial stage is to develop a practical structure of personal possessions and ego boundaries which is realistic and appropriate for spiritual growth. The qualities which make a person an eligible student of Vedanta keep on growing throughout their learning. Several of Vedanta's teachings (especially those of a preparatory nature, including appreciation of the need to live by universal values, proper understanding of God, and the cultivation of an appropriate attitude to the results of an individual's actions) are really designed to increase adhikaritvam. Many practices, such as prayer and some forms of meditation, in the initial stages of Vedantic study also do more in terms of improving eligibility rather than in communicating Vedanta's core teachings. Therefore, just because a person does not meet with the entire list of desired qualities in full, there is no reason to feel disheartened or to hesitate in taking up the study of Vedanta.

In some ways this whole question of adhikaritvam comes up for discussion not only because some eligibility criteria are obviously necessary but also to ensure that there is no false conclusion in the matter of Vedanta being an independent means of knowledge. We have seen that a means of knowledge *must* work in appropriate conditions. In fact, actual knowledge is not will-based nor a matter of choice when all conditions necessary for knowledge to take place are present. Vedanta is a means of knowledge. It *must* work by dispelling self-ignorance in every seeker. However, this of course does not happen and, in fact, most seekers do not reach the ultimate objective of dispelling all ignorance surrounding the self. When Vedanta does not seem to work, the immediate and, perhaps, defensive reaction is that either there is nothing like the real self or that Vedanta is not the means for knowing it. This is where the issue of adhikaritvam—eligibility—becomes important: Vedanta is a means of knowledge for an *eligible* seeker and when it does not work it is because there is need to increase and improve eligibility.

How does a student know whether they have enough eligibility to start the pursuit of Vedanta? The answer is simple and practical. If a person has taken even some interest in Vedanta then there is already an element of eligibility. If they continue to pursue Vedanta and some of its teachings begin to take root and actually start working for them in daily life, even in small measure, then this is a further sign of present and growing eligibility. One of the beauties of Vedanta is that its study continues to increase eligibility, and the beneficial impact of the resulting change in attitudes is felt in all aspects of life even if the seeker does not develop total eligibility or complete the entire journey.

Let us now take a look at a few other matters connected with the topic of the student. One conclusion which is often heard is that people only turn to Vedanta due to great physical or emotional pain or major reverses in life such as the total loss of a fortune or of a reputation. It is true that suffering is a trigger which can prompt a turn to Vedanta. But, often (and increasingly from among a financially successful segment of society in our present times) a surfeit of comforts and apparent security also acts as a trigger;

this is so because, for some people, the contradiction in continuing to feel unfulfilled and wanting amidst plenty provokes questions outside the usual structure of conditioning and objectives.

On the other hand, great misfortunes and great good fortune can also be major obstacles on the path of Vedanta. A person who has gone through extreme suffering is likely to look for quick comfort and instant fixes rather than permanent redemption; their reservoir of resources such as energy, patience, and tenacity is likely to have been depleted and their emotions may largely be charged with anger, bitterness, hostility, and general negativity. Such a person would need a lot of care and compassion along with sufficient time with the preparatory teachings of Vedanta to restore balance to their conscious and subconscious mind; without this preparation, the ultimate message of Vedanta cannot strike home. Similarly, a person who has achieved an exceptional degree of conventional success may have developed, in that process, an aggressive and exploitative approach to everything; success also tends to inflate and strengthen the ego. Such a state is obviously not conducive to learning, where receptivity and humility are necessary.

However, all these are generalizations based on possible tendencies and, like all generalizations, they need not apply to any one specific instance. Human minds are very complex and can change unpredictably; individuals can learn and achieve things which defy usual expectations. While probabilities are useful as guides, they should not be taken as foregone conclusions. People become students of Vedanta for a variety of reasons and progress at widely differing rates in their pursuit.

Another question which often arises is whether children should be made to study Vedanta. Many well-meaning parents with an Indian cultural background reason that if Vedanta is valuable, why not expose children to it as early as possible? Here again some understanding and caution is required. Children who are preteens can and should be exposed to simple religious practices but are undoubtedly too young to be exposed to Vedanta. Teenagers, especially in the late teens, can be exposed to some portions of Vedanta but more in terms of some rational explanations for the need to follow universal values, proper understanding of God and prayers, and the development of an appropriate attitude (based on reason) to the results of any action. However, exposure to further teachings of Vedanta requires a certain amount of maturity which usually comes with age.[30] Vedanta needs a healthy and developed ego to work on and it also requires a collection of life's experiences to make its teachings come alive and relevant; this can usually only happen to a grown-up person who has lived in the world, has worked towards the usual objectives, and has experienced success and failure.

Should a student of Vedanta make their pursuit a full-time or a part-time affair? Here again there cannot be a general answer which will cater to all. A few exceptional young people have a background or a natural tendency which almost relentlessly pushes them towards the study of Vedanta as the only thing which really interests them. Such persons may make Vedanta a full-time pursuit from a very early stage (such as from the end of high school); very often they grow up to become teachers of Vedanta and many may also become sannyasins, or monks. At the other end of the spectrum, some older people at the end of their working careers, who have no other occupation or responsibilities, may also take to the full-time study of Vedanta.

In between these two poles, there would be a large

---

30. Hindu tradition recognizes three types of age or maturity which deserve respect: (i) *vruddhovaya*, or age by passage of time, (ii) *tapovaya*, or age by penance and austerity, and (iii) *jñanovaya*, or age by knowledge and wisdom. Therefore, wisdom and maturity need not always be supported by grey hair!

number of people who want to study Vedanta but do not want to ignore their other commitments or to initially close their other alternatives and options. Such people can be only part-time students of Vedanta. This has many advantages. First, the satisfaction which comes from not forsaking responsibilities to the family and close associates can be an important ingredient in having a settled mind which is fit for study. Then, the ability to practice the teachings of Vedanta in vexing daily situations not only simplifies life but also provides personal confirmation of the value of Vedantic teachings and becomes a source of encouragement. Finally, when a part-time pursuit of Vedanta is selected, the option to make it full-time at an appropriate stage is always open. On the other hand, however, there does come a time in the study of Vedanta when total immersion for a period of time seems necessary so that the teachings can reach a critical mass and make a breakthrough to permeate all aspects of the student's life.

For an average student, a good way to balance the pros and cons of part-time and full-time learning would be to have a daily regime of self-study (using books and tapes) and daily practices like prayer and meditation. A couple of hours need to be devoted to Vedanta every day, at least in the initial stages of learning. If a teacher is conveniently available then this studying could be guided and encouraged by a weekly or a fortnightly session with the teacher; if this is not possible then a weekly meeting with fellow students in the surrounding area to discuss the material studied, to ask questions for resolution of doubts, and to get a feeling of comradeship and encouragement is very useful.[31] While this process is going on, whatever is possible in the situation should be done to meet the teacher as often as possible.

31. In this context, there is a Sanskrit verse which says that only one-fourth of any learning is obtained directly from the teacher; another one-fourth comes from the student's own thinking; yet another one-fourth comes from discussions with fellow students, and the last one-fourth can come only when sufficient time has elapsed.

Finally, all this regular effort should be supplemented with a periodic full-time (and, if possible, residential) program with the teacher, even if it is only for a week or two in a year. This sort of initial approach can be modified and augmented in time as the student's needs and perceptions change.

It is vital to remember that this discussion on whether Vedanta should be pursued on a part-time or a full-time basis has no bearing on the basic attitude of the student, which should be that of a mumukshu at all times. If anybody pursuing Vedanta begins to look at life as being divided into two parts of which one consists of the times when they are a student of Vedanta and the other of the time during which they play their other roles (employee, father, husband, and so on), then a dangerous dichotomy and considerable anguish are likely to follow. This is because the role as the student of Vedanta will come in continuous competition and opposition with the demands and needs of the other roles which the same person plays. After all, for most people the actual time spent in listening to the teacher or reading Vedantic texts will be only a fraction of the time spent on other pursuits. This can result in a feeling of guilt or inadequacy and even lead to resentment towards other roles, which may seem annoying intrusions on limited resources of time and energy. Alternatively, a person can cleverly juggle resources and "fit in" the targeted one hour or two hours of Vedanta as one fits in tennis lessons or visits to the dentist. Unfortunately, neither anger and resentment towards other pursuits and duties nor making Vedanta *one* of the several matters to be skillfully woven into the fabric of a busy daily schedule works effectively for any length of time. In fact, such approaches result in a state of mind which is not at all helpful to the meaningful pursuit of Vedanta.

This, of course, does not mean that no other activities or goals are to be pursued, but it does mean that the primary underlying goal behind each and every role and each and every activity should be increasing eligibility for total liberation. To put this in the form of a simple example, a person who is a mumukshu can take action to increase their money resources by changing to a better-paying job, by starting a new business, or by studying stock markets; simultaneously, they would devote a portion of each day to the study of Vedanta by going to the teacher, reading, and meditating. There is no problem here, even if their money-making activities take up the bulk of their time, as long as they do not begin to value money subjectively and falsely. A mumukshu has the freedom to undertake activities appropriate to their legitimate wants and desires as well as the obligation to fulfill appropriately such roles as may be relevant to their particular life. However, throughout these activities, they must not forget the limited and changeable nature of the usual achievements and gains; consequently, fundamental liberation must remain their primary and permanent goal underlying all other transient and subsidiary goals. Thus, in the pursuit of money, a mumukshu should have no illusions that by finding an appropriate career environment or that by accumulating a certain level of wealth they will be able to address their fundamental problem of being lacking and continuously wanting. The real underlying motivation behind their money-making activities should be to reach a level of financial security which would permit fuller and freer pursuit of self-knowledge or to give vent to their skills and talents, without which a part of their mind is likely to remain unfulfilled and thus become an obstruction during their study and contemplation.

This kind of outlook in all matters (pertaining to security, pleasures, and righteousness) transforms the entire process of living into an integrated and harmonious effort which derives balance and meaning even in trying times due to steady focus on a greater goal which transcends the business of daily living and its inevitable ups and downs. It is this attitude (termed *karma yoga* in the *Bhagavad Gita*) which is vital for all students of Vedanta, irrespective of whether their formal pursuit of Vedanta is full-time or part-time.

Incidentally, and on a more mundane plane, whether the study of Vedanta is undertaken on a part-time or a full-time basis, most people find it valuable to cultivate the habit of actually writing down a periodic summary of whatever has been understood by listening to the teacher, by reading, and by discussions with fellow students; this practice not only provides useful revision but also forces clarity and precision.

Often, a question arises in the mind of a potential or a fresh student of Vedanta regarding the need to be an expert in Sanskrit. As the original texts are all in Sanskrit and Sanskrit is a language which is often not translated well, there are obvious advantages in being personally proficient in Sanskrit. On the other hand, it takes several years of considerable effort before one gains the expertise to mean-ingfully read complex Sanskrit material containing subtle thoughts and implications. Unless one has a flair for language learning or is committed to the full-time pursuit of Vedanta and Sanskrit for several years, one can make steady and significant progress in the study of Vedanta without concerning oneself with the formal learning of Sanskrit. Given a limited amount of time and enthusiasm, I would personally use those resources to understand Vedanta using a familiar language at the initial stages. Later, depending upon personal inclination and need, one can always take up the study of Sanskrit; in any case, many Sanskrit words and phrases, commonly used in Vedanta, become almost effortlessly familiar during the study of Vedanta even in a different language.

Let us now end this section on the student by looking at what has been said about a person who has initial eligibility to study Vedanta but does not make the effort to increase their eligibility and strive for self-knowledge. In this context, verse 5 of the *Vivekachudamani* asks:

itah konavasti mudhatma yastu swarthe pramadhyati durlabham manusham deham prapya tatrapi paurusham.

Is there greater folly than in the person who, having obtained the rare opportunity of a human birth, and that too with the required intellectual and emotional qualities, does not make full effort to understand their own self?

With this, let us now turn to the teacher, without whom our study of Vedanta cannot be undertaken. While we look at the teacher, we will also indirectly look at a few more qualities required of the student in relation to the teacher.

The Teacher

In the entire scheme of Vedanta, the teacher undoubtedly has the pivotal role. Without the appropriate teacher, this timeless wisdom and its teaching methodology are likely to remain sterile even for an eligible student. In fact, the words of the Upanishads become a unique and independent means of knowledge *only* when wielded by the right teacher. Why is this so? What is so special about a teacher of Vedanta? What are the characteristics of a proper teacher of this subject? Does this teacher need to be approached and dealt with differently compared to a teacher of some other subject? Let us try to look into some of these questions in this section.

But before we go further, let us start using the Sanskrit word *guru* instead of the word *teacher*, at least for the rest of this section. The etymological interpretation of this word has a number of different meanings, but we will go with the most commonly accepted variant, which is *remover of darkness.* The word *guru* has now passed into common parlance not only in relation to traditional Indian art forms (such as music and dance) but in almost any field of endeavor (and so we have marketing gurus, management gurus, and the like). However, as mumukshus or seekers of liberation we are interested in the removal of only one kind of darkness, and this is the ignorance covering the true nature of our own self. Therefore, in the context of Vedanta, a guru is described as *mahavakya upadesha karta:* that is, as someone who unfolds the meaning of the great sentences of the Upanishads (such as the equation "You are That," which has been mentioned earlier).

Let us go back to the questions which we raised about the guru. Why is he or she indispensable and so special? The answer lies both in the nature of the subject on which the guru is expected to throw light and in the complex relationship the guru needs to establish and maintain with the student.

The self, which is the guru's subject, is the basis of all knowing and the only invariable presence in all experiences. Other teachers have to teach about physical objects, forces, places, events, processes, relationships, emotions, experiences, and concepts, all of which can be considered as objects in the sense that they are all separate from the consciousness or the cognitivity of the student. The guru's peculiar task is to focus on this consciousness itself, which is the subject and because of which the student cognizes, experiences, and understands anything. The difficulty here is obvious, because how is the student's consciousness to be made conscious of consciousness? Because this cannot be done, the guru's task becomes very unusual and subtle.

A different kind of difficulty arises from the fact that the guru cannot solve the student's problem at the level at which the problem arises. The problem of the student is that their body and mind are mortal, ignorant, and limited and no guru can make their body and mind immortal, all-knowing, and unlimited. The freedom provided by Vedanta is not so much *for* the individual as it is *from* the individual. The guru has to provide initial reassurance by saying that the problem has a solution, but ultimately the guru has to make the student see that the solution lies in understanding that the problem itself is not real. The guru has to make the student understand that consciousness is the real self and that this consciousness is in the nature of sat, chit, and ananda: that is, pure and permanent existence, awareness, and limitlessness. The guru thus has to lead the student to the conclusion that the very notion of bondage and limitation, which has launched the student on the path of self-knowledge, is illegitimate. The guru solves a problem which had no real existence to begin with!

All this seems simple enough. It appears to be a straight-forward matter of reading the Upanishads and some related commentaries; after all, the Upanishads and other texts contain knowledge of the self and there appears to be no particular reason for the role of the guru to be so critical. However, in fact, there are many reasons why knowledge of the Upanishads does not become truly available to most students without a guru. Some of these reasons are:

- Difficulties in drawing proper meaning from the general contents of the Upanishads.
- Problems in making some commonly used words in the texts yield their uncommon meaning.
- The natural tendency of the student to look upon any discussion on the nature of the self as a discussion of something other than *I*—that is, other than the student's own self.
- The importance of arriving at the right balance of efforts between increasing the eligibility of a student and, concurrently, of imparting some of the core teachings of Vedanta.

- The need to have a live example of a person who has completed the Vedantic journey.

Let us take a brief look at these matters.

As we have seen, the Upanishads are written in an archaic language and style. Sanskrit is not the easiest of languages to learn and interpret. Further, even in Sanskrit, the message of the Upanishads is not put forth in an organized and sequential manner. Many statements in the Upanishads are, on the face of it, ambiguous and even contradictory. They were never designed to be read as a structured course but contain vignettes of sublime experiences for the purpose of inspiration and are meant for unfoldment only by a teacher who has also personally been through similar experiences. Quite apart from this, the individual verses of the Upanishads do not convey very much unless they are seen in the context of the total teachings—and the total teachings do not become available unless the individual verses are properly understood! The only way out of this predicament is for the guru, who has the whole vision, to bring out the proper meaning of the individual verses in the correct context of the entire teachings.

The problem of apparently known words used in the Upanishads and other texts is also considerable. Words like *eternal, infinite, immortal, all-pervading* and the like are used. Because these words are part of our everyday vocabulary, it is assumed that their meanings are obvious; however, none of us actually has any clear and direct understanding of their meanings. This is not very surprising—for instance none of us has ever known or experienced anything truly eternal, and so when we use this word we may have an idea of something which stretches over aeons of time, but we are not able to really relate to timelessness. It is for this reason that when we are taught about the self by less than a proper guru, we think we have understood that the atma is eternal and all-pervading—and yet we wonder when and where we will actually find the atma! There cannot, of course, be any *when* or *where* about the eternal and all-pervading. The guru's task is therefore not to describe the atma as eternal and all-pervading but to fully bring out the proper meanings of such words themselves so that they are not seen as some adjectives to an object called atma but as the very nature of the only truth.

A guru has to repeatedly make it clear during the teaching process that what is being discussed is not some different and remote thing but is the very essence of the student, as the student is, here and now. If the guru is not competent and careful, then the student will automatically employ the usual process of subject-object division, whereby the atma, the object, is treated as something to be known by the student, the subject. The moment the atma is understood in the third person (that is, not as the first-person *I* but as the third-person *he* or *she* or *it*), then any teaching about the atma becomes a further superimposition. We do not know the self, and take our body or mind to be our real self. If the atma is sought to be understood *by* us (the ego) as against *being* us, then any knowledge from that perspective only becomes a further layer of information available to be used by the ego in furthering its own agenda and ultimately reinforcing the fundamental problem instead of resolving it. A guru of skill, patience, and compassion is needed to make sure that this does not happen. It is important but difficult to appreciate that the atma is the only invariable presence in our very being and in each one of our experiences and in all our knowing; the guru has to make this understanding clear and vivid.

Yet another unusual feature of the process of Vedantic teaching is the fact that the guru has to not only impart the actual core teachings but also simultaneously guide the student in the concurrent and necessary effort to improve their eligibility to be ready for the teachings. Both these processes have to go on side by side. Here the guru has to judge the conditioning and capacity of the student in order to determine the nature and mix of the teachings appropriate to that student and the pace at which the student should be led. Students come to learn with different levels of intellectual and emotional preparedness; each student also has their own unique collection of wrong notions and different types of conditioning. Emotional maturity requires the healing and discharge of pent-up issues in the conscious and the subconscious mind; it also requires learning to deal with life without a further build-up of unwanted emotions. The guru's work in this area can cover religion, God, death, family, work, money, friends, disease, relationships, fears, hopes, and ambitions. A guru needs to be able to play the role of a parent and a friend, a priest and a psychologist, a person of the world and a philosopher if the guru is to guide the student to maturity and objectivity. In this process the student's many questions need to be answered and the student has to be provided with prescriptions and practices; often, the answers provided to an individual student, and the prescriptions and practices suggested for them by the guru, may have nothing to do with the actual teachings of Vedanta but much to do with the particular mindset and conditioning of that student.

The question of conditioning assumes another and a different kind of importance in our present times. In dealing with some categories of modern students the guru does not have the initial benefit of traditional faith, reverence, and humility from the student. Of course, a true guru does not need these attitudes from students for the guru's sake but for the sake of the students themselves so that they can be open and receptive to the teachings. A compassionate guru has to make a lot of allowance for the prejudices and smugness of some types of students and has to deal with them at their own level of modernity. Unfortunately modernity is often represented by tunnel vision camouflaged as a scientific or a rational way of thinking, and the guru has the additional task of widening the student's field of vision and augmenting their ways of thinking.

Proper timing is also an important judgment to be made by the guru. Not guiding a willing and able student to their full potential is wasteful and frustrating; on the other hand, there is great danger in propelling a student to the further reaches of Vedanta too quickly—this may lead to improper understanding as well as to a dangerous vacuum created by demolishing false but comforting old notions without replacing them with something of more value and validity.

Not only does the guru have to play all these roles and expose the student to various facets of the teachings; the guru also has to do this repeatedly, and following a method. While the methodology is well-established in Vedanta over centuries, the guru needs great patience and skill in wielding this methodology in the context of an individual student with unique needs. And the guru's task does not end with just exposing the student to the entire teachings, because even after that, it is entirely possible for the new understanding not to have much practical effect in the student's daily life. The weight of age-old conditioning and the deep grooves of past thinking modes may lead to the continuation of the student's fundamental problem. Redemption and deliverance may require extended further effort, guided by the guru, for deconditioning and for fully imbibing the teachings in every aspect of living.

There is another rather curious but relevant aspect of the guru which we should look at while we are on the topic of the importance of a guru. This has to do with being in the live, physical presence of the guru. By some inexplicable process or in some unfathomable way, just being in the guru's presence brings about a certain settlement in the state of the qualified student's mind and creates a certain amount of openness, receptivity, and hope. Spending more time with the guru and observing her or him in the various situations of day-to-day living provides further stimulation and encouragement to the student. The words of the Upanishads assume a different kind of liveliness and relevance when personally unfolded by the guru; the ring of truth in the teachings is heard and felt instinctively and unambiguously in the presence of the true guru. The tranquility, the quiet conviction, the healing, and the wholeness felt in association with the guru is a joy and blessing which needs to be actually experienced because, like love, it defies description or explanations. Without this special touch the teachings of Vedanta can remain inert and be ineffective beyond pandering to idle or scholarly curiosity.

Having seen some of the reasons because of which the guru is indispensable, we can now look at what the Upanishads say about a proper guru. Verse I.2.12 of the *Mundaka Upanishad* states:

tadvijñanartham sa gurumevabhighacchet samitpanih shrotriyam brahmanishtham.

Let him [the student], in order to obtain the knowledge of the eternal, take sacrificial fuel in his hands and approach that teacher alone who is well-versed in the Vedas and is established in [committed to] brahman.

The prepared and eligible student is asked to go to a guru with the attitude of humility and service (denoted by the phrase *take sacrificial fuel in his hands*)—but only to a guru who is well-versed in the Vedas *(shrotriya)* and also who is committed to only brahman *(brahmanishtha)*. Why these two qualifications for the guru? Is it not possible for a person to have self-knowledge and teach it without knowing the Vedas? On the other hand, why does a guru who knows the Vedas also have to be established or absorbed in brahman?

There is no doubt that there have been and there will continue to be some persons with true and total self-knowledge (or, more accurately, persons who have no remaining ignorance about their true nature) who have not read the Vedas. The experiences and words of many such persons throughout recorded history have an uncanny similarity with the contents of the Upanishads even though they may have never studied them. Quite a few persons with such wisdom become well-known and are proclaimed as gurus by their associates and admirers. As long as people seeking liberation from their problems look upon such truly accomplished great persons only as symbols to revere and to draw inspiration and comfort from, there is no difficulty. However, an average student of Vedanta is not likely to achieve systematic and complete removal of their self-ignorance only by relying on teachings derived from such persons. This is because the traditional teachings not only contain great truths but also contain equally important methods and well-established processes and practices for guiding students on the path of learning. This entire teaching tradition (termed *sampradaya*) has evolved over centuries; because it is so vital, it is handed down from generation to generation in an unbroken line (termed *parampara*) of traditional teachers of Vedanta. A guru who is not well-versed in the Vedas (which implies both the words of the texts and also the teaching tradition and methodology) is unlikely to be able to effectively unfold this knowledge for the usual student. Hence, the injunction is to go to a guru who is *shrotriya*.

Why the requirement that the guru should be *brahmanishtha*, or committed only to brahman? The crux of

Vedanta's teaching is that brahman is the ultimate reality, that the atma is our real nature, and that brahman and atma are the same, non-dual whole. Anybody who truly understands this teaching can never have any real commitment to anything else because all creation can only be like a shadow of the reality of brahman. The guru certainly plays his role in the game of life and living—the guru lives, teaches, works, and plays and, in many ways, appears to be no different than many of us. However, beneath these superficial actions, no situations, actions, or results of actions (including the success or failure of the teaching) can really affect the guru. If the guru has other commitments and has a personal agenda to fulfill, then the guru too is in the process of becoming—of feeling a lack or a want, of making efforts to overcome that limitation, and thus letting their happiness depend upon the results of their actions in that direction. If this is so, then in terms of self-knowledge such a guru is really as ignorant as the student, even though the guru may have memorized the contents of all the Upanishads. Such a guru can, of course, pass on the words of Vedanta to the student, but because the guru does not feel and actually live the teachings, he or she will never be able to communicate the true and firsthand spirit of the teachings. It is such teachers who, perhaps unknowingly, create subtle wrong impressions in the minds of their students, who then wrongly think of the atma in the third person (as *he* or *she* or *it*).

Based on such wrong impressions, many students wait for some special time or place for the atma to show itself, or look upon the atma as a hidden pearl to be wrested from some mysterious inner recesses of the heart or from underneath the waves of thoughts and emotions. Others believe that the atma is something to be experienced, and hope for fountains of a special brand of bliss to spring up upon reading the Upanishads. As we have seen earlier, the non-dual reality in the nature of sat, chit, and ananda cannot be subject to limitations of time and place; it is the very essence of every *I* and of all thoughts, emotions, experiences, knowledge, and action. There is no hidden atma behind emotions in the heart or behind thoughts in the mind, because emotions and thoughts are nothing but the atma (while the atma, of course, is not confined to only emotions or thoughts). The ananda of the atma is not some bliss or joy to be experienced but a natural fullness or wholeness. For all this to be clearly explained and brought home so that proper understanding is fully integrated with the student's whole personality and life, what is needed is a guru who is a *brahmanishtha*: a living example of the teachings, who teaches based on personal knowledge.

Apart from these traditional qualifications of a guru there are a few other considerations which may be specially relevant here. Let us begin with a mundane but practical consideration, which is the physical location of the guru. When a person wants to study Vedanta along with having a career and a family, they cannot drop everything and rush off to move in with the guru wherever she or he may be. The proximity of the guru becomes a very relevant matter: if the guru is located too far then periodic meetings and guidance become very difficult—but these are crucial, especially in the early stages of learning.

Another factor which does assume importance is the language in which the guru teaches. The Upanishads, as we have seen, are *shabda pramana*, or a means of knowledge by using words; the language in which the guru wields and unfolds these words makes a great difference in their impact on the student. What matters here is not only the basic language in which the guru teaches (say, English) but also the guru's expression, idiom, and fluency. English, for instance, can be used in a stilted, outmoded, and dead manner (one just has to see several translations of beautiful Sanskrit texts completely ruined by jarring renderings into Victorian English); English can also be skillfully used in a lively and contemporary fashion to convey accurate meaning in a manner relevant to current times. In this context, the cultural orientation of the guru may also affect students considerably. Many modern students could be put off at the very outset if the guru adopts a pompously formal and distant style or totally lacks humor; in the same vein, a guru who discourages questions and dialogue is not likely to be effective today because we are no longer willing to receive and accept even true knowledge in the format of a sermon, no matter how fervently and eloquently preached.

Another very important matter which the guru needs to periodically clarify during the process of teaching is the fact that while the Upanishads are the unique and final means of self-knowledge, they are not the ultimate authority in respect of their other contents. The Upanishads contain not only material regarding the true nature of our own self (unfoldment of which is the purpose of the Upanishads) but also a lot of other interspersed material dealing with matters such as the process of creation of this universe, the working of karma, and even the description (!) of the atma. Some of this ancillary material just represents the world-view on that subject at the time when that particular piece of telling or writing occurred. For instance, when the Upanishads talk about the five primal elements (called the *pancha mahabhutas*, which we have seen earlier as *akasha* - space, *vayu* - air, *agni* - fire, *apa* - water, and *prithivi* - earth), they are certainly not to be taken as the final word on this subject. There is no need to throw out Mendeleev's periodic table of elements which we studied as part of high school science. This is because the process of creation of this world and the nature of its constituent elements are *not* the real subject matters of the Upanishads; information dealing with the five primal elements is included in the Upanishads only to complete a possible model needed to deal with the peripheral curiosity of students of ancient times.

The guru also needs to deal with apparent contradictions in the core contents of the Upanishads, such as when the atma is described as if it has attributes like size and location.[32] This is not to be taken literally but to be regarded partly as poetic license and partly as an attempt to progress to the attributeless nature of the atma in gradual steps. If all this is not properly explained by the guru, we could have a situation proverbially described (rather gruesomely!) as throwing the baby out with the bathwater; unless properly guided, a modern student may reject the entire contents of the Upanishads because some peripheral or preliminary contents outrage the student's common sense or do not tally with the student's valid knowledge obtained through other proper means.

How does one go about identifying a proper guru? After all, it is a bit difficult to judge a potential guru as *shrotriya* (well-versed in the Vedas) and *brahmanishtha* (committed only to brahman) when one knows nothing about the Vedas or brahman oneself! Most of us obviously have to rely on the opinions of other persons and on the general reputation of a particular guru; a personal meeting is also likely to lead to useful intuitive conclusions based on perceived behavior, attitudes, and some sort of personal chemistry. Ultimately, one has to make a beginning based on practical judgment which may need to be revised later. Even if one begins with a less than perfect guru, there is always a lot to be learnt. A teacher who has just scholarly knowledge of the Upanishads will certainly not be as

---

32. For instance the *Shvetashvatara Upanishad* (verse 3.13) says: "The purusha [atma], being of the size of the thumb, is concealed by the heart, intellect, and mind and always dwells in the hearts of all beings."

effective as a person who has that knowledge along with personal and direct conviction—but, on the other hand, a great deal about the contents of different types of Vedantic texts can be learnt from a merely scholarly person. There is no reason not to learn whatever one can from an available teacher and begin dealing with a better-qualified guru later, whenever that opportunity arises. At the end of it all, finding a proper guru is not entirely a matter of one's own judgment or effort, and some of this has to be left to luck; after making suitable efforts to find a guru, it is useful to cultivate the faith that whichever force made one into a spiritual seeker will also, at the appropriate time, provide the right guru. One of the very early verses (verse 3) of the *Vivekachudamani* states:

durlabham trayamevaitdevanugrahahetukam manushy-atvam mumukshutvam mahapurushsamshrayah.

Three rare things become available only due to divine grace: humanhood, the desire for fundamental libera-tion, and the shelter of a great person.

Apart from the good luck in being born a human being and developing a longing for real freedom, this verse talks about the good fortune in finding a true guru. This fortune is not only in terms of finding a great person who can teach and protect the student with proper knowledge of reality but also in terms of the student being able to recognize and surrender their ego to such a guru.

To find a true guru is a great blessing—and there is further great blessing involved in recognizing that the finding of a true guru is a great blessing!

With this look at the guru, let us now turn to the teaching methodology employed by a proper teacher of Vedanta.

The Teaching Methodology

How does Vedanta teach? Where is the long-established teaching tradition of Vedanta codified? Is there any teaching methodology in the Upanishads themselves? The answers to questions like this may not be obvious during the initial acquaintance with Vedanta. Vedanta's teaching methodology is not separately spelt out in any one Upanishad but is spread, directly and indirectly, over all the Upanishads. In many ways the teaching method is inseparable from an individual teacher because each teacher wields the words of the Upanishads in a uniquely personal way. As we saw earlier in the section on "The Teacher," it is the teacher who has the essential and subtle task of unfolding and conveying uncommon meaning from the common words used in Vedanta's texts. However, leaving aside the role of the all-important teacher, the Upanishads themselves do contain an effective process of teaching. This teaching process is further amplified in some subsequent Vedantic texts. However, we will only look at some of what is contained in the Upanishads themselves, and that too only in relation to imparting its core teachings.

There are several aspects to this teaching methodology, but these apparently different aspects and sub-processes really fit in together to form a beautifully unified and effective way of conveying the teachings of the Upanishads. The teaching process has to create an appropriate environment and attitude for learning; it has to take into account the way in which the human mind functions and imbibes knowledge; it has to recognize that seekers will approach Vedanta with varying amounts of preparation and different layers of conditioning; it has to reckon with the fact that many seekers will not complete the entire journey. The teaching process also has to deal with the fundamental difficulty that the object on which the light of knowledge is to be cast is itself the ultimate subject *I* because of whom all knowing is possible. Let us briefly examine how some such issues are addressed by the teaching methodology in the Upanishads.

All Upanishads begin with a *shanti patha* (peace invocation) with the intention of creating the right frame of mind for learning. An example of a well-known *shanti patha* is found, amongst other places, at the beginning of the *Katha Upanishad*:

> *om! saha navavatu. saha naubhunaktu.*
> *saha viryam karvavahai. tejasvinavadhitamastu.*
> *ma vidvishavahai. om! shanti. shanti. shantih.*

> May He protect us (both student and teacher). May He nourish us. May we acquire the capacity to exert (in the study of scriptures). May our study be brilliant (leading to proper understanding). May we (student and teacher) not have discord. May we have peace in all aspects of life.

Recitation of verses such as these, sitting appropriately before the teacher and in the right sort of environment, brings about a certain settlement of other distracting thoughts and emotions running in the mind. The opening invocation—*om!*—seeks God's help in all humility. This particular verse also warns against the possible tendency of students to unnecessarily disagree with the teacher because of trifling objections and false or quibbling arguments.

In order to convey their actual message, the Upanishads do not only rely on bare statements of facts and experience but couch many of the teachings in the format of questions and answers as well as stories and examples. This approach anticipates questions likely to occur to many students and provides answers of increasing depth and subtlety, mirroring the progression of actual learning in a student. By using stories and examples from daily experience, the teaching method tries to provide familiar and stable ground from which to launch the flight into the unknown and the sublime. Exhortation and encouragement are provided from time to time and specific sub-processes for learning are set out.

Let us look at something which is partly an exhortation to a student but contains a very important learning process. This is a line from the *Brihadaranyaka Upanishad*:

atma vare drishtavyah shrotavyo mantavyo nidhidhy-asitavyah.

Atma has to be seen (known) by listening, reflecting, and meditating.

The three steps of *listening, reflecting,* and *meditating* are well-established in the process of teaching Vedanta. The student first needs to be exposed to the teachings by *listening* to the teacher and undergoing a process of self-inquiry guided by the teachings as heard from the teacher. Next follows *reflection*, which really refers to resolving doubts caused in the student's mind by the teachings. Personal conviction can be brought about only by thinking, by bringing up doubts and then getting them satisfactorily resolved. Without this process the initial teachings would remain only superficial and secondhand information. The last step, *meditation*, is to repeatedly practice and experience the effect of some of the teachings which have been heard and have been cleared of intellectual doubts. (An example here could be a daily period of meditation wherein a person just quietly watches their own body and mind— they become an uninvolved and unresisting witness to all physical sensations as well as mental movements such as the arising of memories, associations, and thoughts. This is only one illustration of a type of practice which brings home the teaching that an individual is more than just the body or the mind.)

This kind of effort is needed not only to assimilate what one has learnt; its repeated practice is essential to counteract the wrong notions (that one is the body or the mind) which have been deeply established by initial ignorance and years of conditioning. This entire process, often referred to as *shravana-manana-nidhidhyasana*[33] *(listening-reflecting-meditating)*, is essential and needs a certain amount of time for it to work. Also, this process is not sequential—we cannot finish all listening first and then start thinking about what we have heard. As we meditate and reflect upon whatever we have learnt, we continue to listen and to learn more and more. Further, even the listening or learning with regard to any one aspect of the teachings is not a one-shot affair. Given the nature of the subject of the teaching and the quality of surrounding ignorance, it is necessary for students to expose themselves to the teachings again and again. Repetition, different frames of mind of the student, and different words used by the teacher at different times, as well as the passage of time, all lead to the opening of small and occasional chinks in the layers of conditioning surrounding the student, with the possibility of some teachings penetrating and finding their mark.

We saw earlier that for the purpose of making the student understand some of its teachings in different perspectives,

---

33. It is pertinent to note that for many people who take some interest in Vedanta, their pursuit never really progresses beyond the listening and reading stage. Because of pressures on time and difficulty in having regular association with a good teacher, people often tend to go to sporadic lectures and do random reading. Even regularly attending several public discourses by the same teacher has limitations because whenever a teacher is dealing with a heterogeneous group, the teaching tends to be pitched at the lowest common denominator. While all such inputs are good, progress does require bringing in reflection and meditation by deliberate effort.

the teaching methodology of Vedanta uses several different frames and examples from our daily experiences. Each such perspective is used as a method to communicate some aspect of the teachings and is called a *prakriya* (method). I will mention a few of these, starting with the *pancha kosha prakriya*. *Pancha* means *five* and *kosha* means *sheath;* this particular method is an analysis of the five sheaths which are mistaken for the real *I* or which are thought to apparently cover the atma. The five sheaths are:

- The physical body (which causes us to say "*I* am tall" or "*I* am male").
- Life-forces and processes (which cause us to say "*I* am hungry" or "*I* am breathless").
- Emotions (we all feel and say "*I* am angry" or "*I* am happy").
- Thinking, including the *I*-thought or ego (which gives us the sense of individuality, and we then feel or say "*I* am the doer/knower/enjoyer").
- A state of temporary suspension of individuality (such as in deep sleep, which is a restful experience because problems caused by a sense of individuality do not intervene).

All these five states are carefully analyzed in the Upanishads and it is shown that none of them is the real *I*.

Another well-known *prakriya* is the *avasthatraya prakriya*, which looks into three different states known to all human beings. These are the states of waking, dreaming, and deep sleep. It is shown that when awake, the individual seems far removed from the status of a dreamer or a sleeper; when in a dream, the same individual is alive only to their dream world; when in deep sleep, the same person has no attributes of the dreamer or the awake person. These three states are not only mutually exclusive: they replace each other in a continuing cycle. Because anything which is real cannot give up its intrinsic reality at any time and because a real backdrop is needed for a continuously changing state to exhibit itself, it is shown that none of the three states of waking, dreaming, or sleeping can be the ultimate reality.

Yet another way of looking at things is the *karana-karya prakriya*, which is an analysis of causes and effects. Every effect has a cause. Thus, the cause of a shirt is its fabric (and, in a different way, the shirtmaker or tailor). The weight and color of the shirt are nothing but the weight and color of the fabric, and while we can have the fabric without a shirt, we cannot have a shirt without the fabric. Therefore, in a way, it could be said that the fabric (the material cause) has a higher level of reality: the shirt (the effect) is dependent on the fabric, but the fabric is independent of the shirt. However, it is not that the shirt is unreal—the shirt is evident to us and is of great practical use. Now if the fabric is more real than the shirt but the shirt is also real in its own way, then we have a problem of terminology. This problem is solved by having three different terms, which do not force us to classify things only as *real* or *unreal* but also provide a third category. So, in Sanskrit, we have not only the term *satyam*, which means *that which exists*, and *tuccham*, which means *that which does not exist* (like a circular triangle or the child of a barren woman), but also *mithya*, which is used to denote things which have a *dependent existence*.

In our fabric/shirt analogy, the fabric would be *satyam*,[34]

---

34. The fabric can be called *satyam* only for the limited purpose of this fabric-shirt example. From the perspective of the yarn from which the fabric is made, the fabric would be *mithya* and the yarn would be *satyam*. One could go further and further back, terming each more fundamental constituent as *satyam*, until one comes to the smallest subatomic particle currently known to science. We can then wait for science to discover an even more fundamental particle—or be open to the possibility that all matter and all energy is only a manifestation of consciousness.

but the shirt cannot be classified as *tuccham* (because it does exist); it is to be regarded as *mithya*, because it has no existence which is independent of the fabric. *Mithya* is in the nature of a name and form *(nama rupa)* attributed to an underlying reality—thus a shirt is nothing but the name given to fabric in a particular form. The fabric is the substantive, while the shirt is in the nature of an attribute to that substantive. However, in our conditioned way of thinking and speaking, we inverse this real state of affairs. Assuming that our shirt is made of cotton fabric, we would say *cotton shirt* and make *shirt* the noun or the substantive and make cotton the adjective or the attribute. In fact *shirt* is *not* the substantive, and truth would be better conveyed by saying *shirty (!) cotton.* (The point here is not to suggest that we should adopt some startling ways of speaking— what is important is the understanding of the reality in a situation). The *karana-karya prakriya* says that the whole world (that is, the entire creation, including us, the individuals) exists and its existence is evident to us. Anything which comes into existence has to be created and is in the nature of a result or an effect of an underlying cause. So, just as the shirt is *mithya* and fabric is *satyam*, so also the entire creation is *mithya* and whatever may be the underlying cause (termed *brahman*) is *satyam*.[35]

---

35. But here our shirt analogy runs into a problem. To obtain the result of a shirt we need both the fabric (the material cause) *and* the shirtmaker (the instrumental or efficient cause). It is also obvious that the instrumental cause must have knowledge of the result— a shirtmaker who does not know what a shirt is would have difficulty in actually making a shirt! It therefore follows that the instrumental cause or maker of the entire creation must also have knowledge of the entire creation. Because knowledge is only compatible with consciousness, it further follows that this all-knowing maker must itself be a conscious being. Now our conscious and knowledgeable shirtmaker had to reach out and get some fabric for creating a shirt. Where and to whom should the creator of everything reach out to obtain material for the entire creation? Prior to creation, nothing is available because nothing has been created. The only possibility here is that, unlike the example of the shirt, the instrumental cause and the material cause of the entire creation which we behold are one and the same! This sounds incredible, because how can the shirtmaker and the fabric be the same thing? A better feel for the possibility of this type of creation can, perhaps, be had when we look at all that we create in our own individual dreams. We can dream of

There are many other examples and prakriyas used by Vedanta, and we obviously cannot look at all of them here. It also has to be remembered that no one example or prakriya is meant to convey Vedanta's full message. But much more important than the consideration of any specific method is the appreciation of the fact that the few methods which we have briefly looked at, and the many more which have not even been mentioned here, all contain a very important common feature: none of them tell the full truth! In fact they all suggest or imply things which are actually false! This sounds both startling and disturbing. After all, the last thing that one would expect from a body of revered, ancient wisdom is half-truths or falsehoods. Why should Vedanta do this? The answer to this is to be found in understanding the real and fundamental teaching methodology of Vedanta, which overrides all subsidiary methods, including the few prakriyas which we have just seen.

What is this fundamental teaching methodology of Vedanta? Let us hear it in the words of Shankara himself (from his bhashya on verse 13, chapter 13 of the *Bhagavad Gita*):

> For there is this saying of those who know the true tradition, "That which cannot be expressed (in its true form directly) is expressed (indirectly) through false attribution and subsequent retraction."

This method of false attribution followed by retraction underlies all forms of Vedanta teachings and is used in

---

nothing other than what we already know in our waking state (even though that knowledge may have been obtained from movies seen when awake and even though we may rearrange and juxtapose bits of what we already know into seemingly original dream creations). Further, we do not reach outside of ourselves for the material to make our dream mountains, dream cities, and dream people. We are both the instrumental and the material causes of our dream creations, which are only manifestations of our own consciousness. This opens up the possibility of the entire creation being a manifestation in and of an all-encompassing consciousness.

different forms throughout the Upanishads, the *Brahma Sutras*, and the *Bhagavad Gita*. It is necessary to do this because there is no way in which the absolute reality, which is the subject matter of Vedanta, can be directly expressed in its true form. It was briefly mentioned in chapter 3 of this book ("The Teachings") that Vedanta's core teachings can be summarized in a *mahavakya* such as *tat tvam asi*, which means "You are That." In that chapter we looked at some length into the truth behind *You* being the atma. We went on to say (without going into any details) that Vedanta does not stop at only understanding the real nature of *You* but goes on to also unfold the true nature of *That*, which is the whole world perceived by any individual. We ended by saying (again without going into any explanations) that Vedanta goes on even further to establish the unity behind the apparently separate realities underlying both *You* and *That* and brings us to advaita— the non-dual fundamental reality labeled *brahman*. How does anyone deal with or speak about or explain a unity which is so basic, so complete that *all* duality is ruled out? In an absolutely non-dual state, can there be any *one* to teach the *other*?

Words and thoughts can deal only with nouns (objects), adjectives, relationships, or activities—how can words (or thoughts) deal with an all-encompassing unity? This absolute and non-dual reality cannot be an object (because there can be no *other* subject to perceive or know it as a separate object), nor an adjective (there is no other to distinguish it from), nor a relationship (relate to what or to whom?), nor an activity (an all-pervading absolute unity cannot be taken anywhere or be made into anything different). In a sense, any single word or even a single thought represents an apparent departure from brahman—because who can speak of or think about anything without a subject-object duality? Vedanta texts contain a story about a qualified student requesting his teacher to teach him about the self. In the story, this teacher maintains his silence in spite of repeated requests for knowledge by the student. Finally he tells the student "I *am* telling you, but you do not understand. This self is utter silence." However, as teaching by silence is not likely to be effective for most people, Vedanta uses the method of false attribution followed by retraction.

Imaginary characteristics are first attributed to the absolute reality, to negate whatever is incompatible with those characteristics; subsequently, even the falsely attributed characteristics are negated. For instance, in the *karanakarya prakriya*, which was our last example of some specific teaching methods, brahman was apparently to be seen as the cause of this entire creation. The purpose of suggesting such a thing is to make sure that brahman is not understood as an effect of any other cause. Later, the real position is clarified in the Upanishads themselves by stating that brahman is *neither an effect nor a cause*. Similarly, when Vedanta texts falsely suggest that the atma (or brahman) is something to be attained or known, they do so to emphasize that only the absolute reality is worth knowing. When the atma is spoken of as "the knower," this too is false, and the purpose is only to clarify that the atma is not an object of our knowing. Later, the implication that the atma is a knower (in the sense of an individual performing the activity of knowing) is displaced by calling the atma only a witness. However, ultimately even witnesshood has to be denied because that too involves some individuation and duality. This is done by saying at several places in the Upanishads that *This self is neither this nor that*. The only reality (within and without everything and everybody) cannot be anything which is conceived by the mind; whatever is taught about it in a positive sense can only be false attributions, and the only thing which can actually be said about it is that *it is neither this nor that*. Incidentally, it is this impossibility of saying anything directly about the main subject which makes Vedanta teachers and books seem full of words without, apparently, quite getting to the point.

This fundamental method of false attribution followed by retraction is not only inevitable because of the nature of knowledge sought to be conveyed by Vedanta; it also has an accompanying benefit of gradual progression. This process does not completely destroy an individual's existing foundation of notions and beliefs at the very outset; instead, it goes in gradual steps, whereby as each false notion is removed, it is replaced with something of greater and more lasting value. This not only is useful for the purpose of proper learning but also benefits those who stop their pursuit of Vedanta midway.

While on the subject of teaching methodology, one often hears of well-known saints who have arrived at true under-standing of the nature of their own self without going through any scriptures or any formal teaching process. One also hears of wonderful changes occurring to people after sitting in silence in a sage's presence or on hearing a single phrase (like a mantra) or after going into a trance. Several others believe that total devotion to God (in whichever form they conceive) is the only way to obtain the real truth. These are difficult issues to deal with, and just because some of these happenings and beliefs may defy common understanding does not necessarily make them untrue or impossible. However, when we study Vedanta we cannot realistically expect to obtain some mysterious shortcut which will permit us to emulate the examples of a few rare persons. After all, if we start to study the composition of classical Western music, our focus should be to learn music composition from its well-established teaching methods and not to get too concerned about how Mozart, for instance, as a five-year-old prodigy, composed his first piece of music.

What about total devotion to God as a means of self-knowledge? The ability to completely surrender to God is both beautiful and helpful. Bhakti brings out a whole host of gentler and nobler aspects of any human being; it also brings about a subsidence of the ego, as the individual's strong sense of separation gets merged into whichever form of God is perceived. A few very well-prepared and receptive individuals in the highest state of devotion may need only a single (and, perhaps, inadvertently obtained) spark of knowledge to light the fire required to dispel ignorance. For some others, given their emotional and intellectual make-up, devotion may be the only way in which they can express their search for meaning, whether or not this leads to full understanding of reality. However, when we look at Vedanta we are looking at a means of knowledge which must function every time and in all cases, and that too in a comprehensible and non-miraculous way (provided the criteria for its functioning have been met). In this context mysterious happenings can only be interesting detours, and while devotion is an essential way of preparation and of living, it cannot be consistently used as a substitute for a knowledge-based methodology.[36]

One last thing which needs to be mentioned in the context of Vedanta's teaching methodology is that an

---

36. Having said this, I would again like to emphasize that Vedanta's knowledge will not bring about the desired change in understanding unless the mind being exposed to Vedanta is fully prepared. Preparation of the mind includes dealing with and adequately processing emotions and issues in both the conscious and subconscious parts of the mind. As we have seen in earlier chapters, a personally acceptable understanding of God is necessary to discharge negative emotions, to heal past and present hurts, and generally to create emotional space and freedom to handle life. For this purpose, to have a notion of God in the sense of some sort of an intellectual abstraction is quite meaningless. As a very crucial part of the preparation for being eligible to receive Vedanta's core teachings, it is necessary, for most of us, to spend the time and effort to cultivate a quality of real communication with God; a vital aspect of such communication is that it must permit the flow of emotions.

attempt to segregate the methods of teaching from the teachings themselves may convey the impression that the teaching process is a finite and impersonal path which connects the seeker and the sought. While in the early stages of exploring Vedanta many of us may find some separate understanding of the teaching process useful, it is important to remember that what makes Vedanta unique is that it is not yet another "becoming" or "getting there" but a discovery of what we already are. Nothing is actually needed to make us or to take us to what we, in fact, always have been. Therefore, though Vedanta's teachings may seem to contain a process, it is a process which gradually cancels itself out. In some ways, however mysterious or meaningless this may sound, Vedanta is a journey which ends where it begins. As we discover this startling truth it is important not to let the mechanics, the length, and the pace of the "process" of learning Vedanta detract from the joy of this apparent but marvelous journey.

The Results

In this chapter we have so far spoken of the student, the teacher, and the teaching methodology of Vedanta. Before we end this chapter it would seem appropriate to take a look at the results when a duly qualified student is taught by a proper teacher using established methodology. Here we must remind ourselves that Vedanta is a means of knowledge. When a means of knowledge operates in the appropriate situation, it brings about a knowing or an understanding which was previously absent. Vedanta, too, operates like this and brings about a cognitive change. Where Vedanta has worked fully, this change in under-standing is total (that is, not subject to any doubts) and permanent (that is, not capable of being covered or undone). Incidentally, it is possible for understanding to be total, in the sense of being free of doubts, but yet not be permanent. This is because years of strong past conditioning may continue to work for some time, even after understanding, to obscure and render inoperative the new understanding; such a state may be close to but is not quite the transformation envisioned by Vedanta.

What is this total and permanent understanding all about? The only understanding can be with regard to the wrong notions that one has carried and cherished about one's own self and has then extended to everything and everyone else. When the atma is the only reality and is itself in the nature of sat, chit, and ananda, then the whole struggle to preserve life, fight ignorance, and obtain happiness becomes a mere game, and that too only at the level of the body and mind. It is not that the body and mind are now seen as *anatma* (meaning *other than atma*), because there is nothing but the atma; the understanding is that while the body and mind are nothing but the atma manifested in a certain form, the atma itself is not only the body or mind; it is, therefore, not to be defined or affected by the successes and failures at the body-mind level. As the mind includes the ego, from which springs the *I*-sense, this understanding also puts our usual notion of individuality and free will into their proper place.

A person who has completed the entire journey of Vedanta and is established in the understanding which Vedanta provides is referred to by various terms, including *jñani, mukta, sthitaprajña, enlightened, realized,* and *free.* The profound realization of the atma as one's true nature produces a sense of inner freedom, fearlessness, and joy, arising from the knowledge that the atma is forever free (not being subservient even to God) and beyond causation or destruction.

A jñani is a totally objective person. However, contrary to popular belief, such a person need not and cannot completely give up a functional sense of individuality when interacting with the world, in spite of realizing that all that there is, is the atma as the non-dual reality. A jñani will eat, sleep, plan their activities, and respond when someone calls their name, just as any other human being. A jñani's body will feel painful and pleasurable sensations; their mind will experience emotions and will have preferences (including, in some cases, preferences for a cigarette or for an alcoholic drink or for non-vegetarian food).[37]

Where the jñani will differ from the rest of us will be in the core of their own awareness or consciousness, which now never gets fully identified with the body and mind. With the freedom and space which become available on disidentification, the body and mind (with their combined ability to experience sensations, to have emotions, to have preferences, to act, and to have a sense of individuality) become privileges, and life itself becomes an interesting interlude for all these faculties to play the field. Most of us can go to a movie and permit a certain amount of identification with the characters and events on the screen so that the show can be enjoyed, and yet retain a distance and an unaffected sense of reality. Similarly, a jñani can enjoy life without losing touch with their own truth; they can interact with the world and other people in spontaneous freedom arising from the knowledge that all seemingly individual actions are really a play of a common, unchanging, and impersonal consciousness. They can afford to have preferences because for them preferences never become compulsions and the activities of the body and mind do not remain a basis for judging the unchanging true self.

The understanding that the doings of my body and mind are not *my* doings cannot just stop there but must lead on to the corollary that the doings of any other person's body and mind are also not *their* doings. Even with this

---

37. Such proclivities are unlikely in a jñani who has been through the full course of traditional Vedanta preparation and learning.

understanding, the day-to-day behavior of the jñani may continue as if the jñani and other people are separate individuals, but this is only a concession to practicality. In fact, with the jñani's own sense of individuality continuing only as a functioning necessity and with other people's driving sense of individuality being seen for the error that it is, the jñani can go through life without the pride, guilt, and enmity from which the rest of us suffer because we take our ego (and other people's egos) as the real *I*.

The equanimity of a jñani, their composure in the face of changing currents of life, and their indifference to concerns and issues which whip up emotions in and actions from others may be mistaken for inertness, insensitivity, and laziness. There are, as we all know, many people who are physically slothful, emotionally insensitive, and intellectually dull. Superficially some of their actions and reactions (or lack thereof) may seem to resemble a jñani's behavior. However, many of the core teachings of Vedanta have little validity or relevance for someone of diminished sensitivity and acuity. After all, there is a vast gulf between a person who is incapable of mourning and someone else who transcends mourning as a result of proper understanding while retaining the emotional potential to feel deep grief. A jñani's equanimity is not a result of heaviness and deadening which makes disequilibrium difficult; a jñani's equanimity arises from knowledge and objectivity, which in fact quicken their perceptions and sharpen their sensitivity.

To get away from some more stereotyped images, a jñani need not be a sannyasin—that is, a jñani can have a family, wear normal clothes, and need not sport flowing hair or have a beard! Also, they need not be a writer of books or a teacher of Vedanta. In fact, they can appear so ordinary that most people may not even know that the jñani is one of the rare ones who have pursued and completed the entire journey of Vedanta. The only visible signs of their knowledge and understanding may be a certain poise, naturalness, and spontaneity; a non-defensive cheerfulness; a light touch in dealings with others; a gentle kindliness which is perceptive but not intrusive or sentimental; an increased generosity of spirit which is unsanctimonious and non-evangelical.

Let us now turn our attention away from the jñani and consider the beneficial results of Vedanta for even those of us who have not completed the full course. As we get further and further into the teachings of Vedanta, the first inkling that there is more to life and to our own self than what we had ever imagined brings about a great sense of hope and purpose. As it dawns upon us (even temporarily, such as during periods of meditation) that our reality goes beyond our body and mind, there is a sense of freedom and an increased sense of understanding and acceptance of people and events around us. As we begin to understand the inherent tendency of our body and mind to try to overcome their own limitations, and the ultimate futility of efforts in this direction, we gain a new perspective from which to view not only our usual efforts but also the efforts of those around us. Very often this kind of understanding makes us into non-judgmental and empathetic listeners to whom people instinctively turn for help and advice. Further, some initial understanding and its effects provide reaffirmation of the validity and efficacy of the teachings of Vedanta, and this generates greater enthusiasm and commitment.

Some other results of the partial and superficial understanding of Vedanta's teachings can be a bit unsettling to begin with. Some people, as they start imbibing the initial concepts and terminology of Vedanta, tend to develop a certain amount of arrogance based on self-righteousness or pseudo-intellectualism, or both. A patronizing attitude may also develop from the notion that Vedanta is the elite primacy which includes all other religions and philosophies and then transcends them. Some others, who may already have other significant intellectual attainments, can make Vedanta into just another scholarly pursuit; they end up reading more and more scriptures, remembering reams of Sanskrit mantras and *shlokas*, and entering into interminable arguments on obscure and controversial points without ever letting the true feel and spirit of Vedanta enter their own lives. Unfortunately, while some familiarity with the scriptures is useful, being a Vedantic scholar is quite different from learning the message of Vedanta; here, any learning which does not work in everyday life and in every moment of living is no learning.

There is a completely different type of problem which may arise, especially with the family, friends, and close associates of the student of Vedanta. Even at the preparatory stage of learning, a certain sense of discrimination and dispassion tends to develop in the student, who may then begin to raise uncomfortable questions or express unpalatable opinions; these could relate to behavior, attitudes, and goals which others in the student's social milieu consider normal, and which perhaps the student had previously espoused. The student may also appear indifferent to company and pastimes which they had once enjoyed and may seem strangely reticent and unmoved in the face of several events affecting themselves and others around them. All this can be very trying for others, who may be justifiably confused and even pained. All that can be said here is that as the student's learning progresses, people around may begin to understand the reasons for and the nature of the change which that individual is undergoing and, ultimately, see the value of that change not only for the student but also even for those around the student.

In this context it also needs to be said that the worthiest of goals—knowledge of the self leading to freedom and tranquility—does demand objective assessment and even sacrifice in the area of our close relationships and associations. In the process of becoming proficient in the art of living with wisdom, there may be need to reconsider whom one associates with. Our friends and associates need to be, by and large, worthy people whose influence (by their habits, values, and behavior) elevates us instead of reinforcing ignorant and slovenly habits which impede our growth.

Much before we come to the results and benefits of the core teachings of Vedanta, we experience significant merit and gain at the earlier preparatory stage. Cultivating an attitude of gratitude and devotion based on a meaningful understanding of God provides relief and composure at the level of emotions. On the day-to-day plane, a combination of admitting God into our life and a realistic understanding of our authorship only of actions but not of their results brings about a sea change in our attitude to successes and failures. More objective understanding of those we deal with resolves a number of problems in interpersonal relationships because human behavior is understood in a different perspective, and many previously vexing issues lose their validity or relevance. A person who has become adept at living in keeping with only some of Vedanta's preparatory teachings can be a very successful and largely happy person. There is a poem by Rudyard Kipling titled "If"[38] which is as good a description as any of someone who has learnt the right attitude to actions and results (often termed *karma yoga*). I would like to share this poem with you:

---

38. As a matter of interest, Rudyard Kipling wrote another poem called "If (For Girls)" wherein the list of desirable qualities and attitudes is much less serious and, presumably, more girlish! It just goes to show the kind of things which were done before male chauvinism was recognized and highlighted!

If

If you can keep your head when all about you
Are losing theirs and blaming it on you;
If you can trust yourself when all men doubt you,
But make allowance for their doubting too;
If you can wait and not be tired by waiting,
Or being lied about, don't deal in lies,
Or being hated, don't give way to hating,
And yet don't look too good, nor talk too wise;
If you can dream—and not make dreams your master;
If you can think—and not make thoughts your aim,
If you can meet with Triumph and Disaster
And treat those two impostors just the same;
If you can bear to hear the truth you've spoken
Twisted by knaves to make a trap for fools,
Or watch the things you gave your life to, broken,
And stoop and build 'em up with worn-out tools;
If you can make one heap of all your winnings
And risk it on one turn of pitch-and-toss,
And lose, and start again at your beginnings
And never breathe a word about your loss;
If you can force your heart and nerve and sinew
To serve your turn long after they are gone,
And so hold on when there is nothing in you
Except the Will which says to them: "Hold on!"
If you can talk with crowds and keep your virtue,
Or walk with Kings—nor lose the common touch,
If neither foes nor loving friends can hurt you,
If all men count with you, but none too much;
If you can fill the unforgiving minute
With sixty seconds' worth of distance run,
Yours is the Earth and everything that's in it,
And—which is more—you'll be a Man, my son!

In Conclusion

◆

HAVING COME TO THE END of this book, let us briefly try to review the purpose and need for Vedanta in our lives. This, of course, will be in the nature of some repetition, but then as we have seen, repetition is very much part of the time-tested teaching methodology of Vedanta. Going over some of the ground which we have already covered but using different words and different methods of expression can make a surprising difference in the amount and quality of our understanding.

Let us begin our review with some basics. Each one of us is born ignorant. Our ignorance at birth is of two types: ignorance about the world, and ignorance of our own self. As we grow, our mind and senses develop: sense perceptions bring in data, associations begin to register, memory grows, and the ability to make inferences and presumptions increases. All these become means of knowledge and we begin to shed our initial ignorance. But what ignorance do we shed? We can shed ignorance about only those objects which can come within the ambit of our means of knowledge.

Our usual means of knowledge are our five senses and the mind, which in combination equip us with the physical and mental faculties of perception, inference, and presumption.[39] Using these faculties we learn about objects, concepts, processes, places, and other people; we also learn about our own body, emotions, intellect, and ego. All these

---

39. To complete the traditional list of the usual means of knowledge, we also have the ability to know by the use of correlative knowledge (that is, by similes and examples) and the ability to know by the knowledge of absence (that is, to know that something or somebody is not present).

are matters which can be objectified—that is, made into mental objects for us, the subject, to understand by using our faculties. This, in turn, means that anything which does or can come within the ambit of our faculties and about which we can gain any understanding *cannot* be the real us. After all, how can the real *I*, who is the witness of the faculties which bring knowledge, *itself* become an object for those faculties, to be grasped and understood by them?

The inevitable conclusion is that by using our usual means of knowledge we can shed our initial ignorance only about the world and never about our real nature. Thus, in our ordinary process of growth from an ignorant newborn to a mature adult, there is a glaring omission—we strive to shed our ignorance, but all our efforts can have an impact only on our ignorance concerning anything and everything other than our own self. We can, therefore, easily go from birth to death with our initial self-ignorance completely untouched and intact, even though we may have made great progress in demolishing our ignorance of other objects and ideas. We can live, love, write poetry, understand our own anatomy and psychology, explore the skies, unravel the mysteries of subatomic particles, put up empires, institutions, and structures, be kind, generous, and religious—and yet not have a single clue about our own essence. How are we to shed this self-ignorance? This is where Vedanta comes in as a unique means of knowledge—knowledge for knowing that knower within us because of whom everything else is known.

At this stage one could raise three different types of doubts or questions:

- Is there really a "self" which is my true essence and which is different from what I already know myself to be?
- Is Vedanta really the means for knowing this self?

- Is there any great merit or purpose in trying to know and understand this real self?

The answer common to all these three questions is an unequivocal *Yes*. Let us try to go over some of the reasoning for this answer.

Let us begin with the first question *(Is there really a "self". . . ?)*. Here the rationale for the affirmative answer *has* to be indicative rather than complete and final. The reasons for this are fairly simple. A conclusive answer to this question can come only when we truly stop considering our body, emotions, intellect, and ego as our true self. This cannot happen at the initial stage unless Vedanta is capable of completing its task in a few short paragraphs of writing. Unfortunately Vedanta does not possess this capacity, and works fully only for a qualified student who needs both a teacher and a certain passage of time. Therefore we cannot have the desired certainty and reassurance in full measure as we start.

However, we need not begin our study of Vedanta as a shot in complete darkness. If our real self is different from our body and mind, then this real self must indicate itself and exhibit its difference from anything else, known or knowable, by being *self-evident*. In fact, our real self *has to be the only self-evident thing*, by which everything that we know becomes known or evident. And we all do know of one self-evident fact for which we need no inputs from our physical and mental faculties, for which we need no outside opinions or confirmation, and about which we never have any doubts or hesitation. This is our own sense of existence, the sense of just *I am*. This constant, unchanging, and independent knowledge of one's own being throughout all ages, states, and situations is the only personal indication we have of the self within us which is different from all that is usually known or knowable. It is this real self within us which enlivens our physical and mental faculties. Lack of a readily available means of knowledge which can remove our innate ignorance about our real nature keeps this vital area in darkness. And, ironically, this is so even though the self is the *only invariable presence* in all our doing, thinking, and knowing. It is, therefore, very important to think about and recognize the relevance of the sense of just *I am* as the only indication we can have at the beginning of our journey to shed self-ignorance.

We must not take this indication lightly, because it is the vital starting capital in our venture. The object which we are seeking to understand in our quest is our own true self. Because this object is also the subject, it cannot be objectified and brought within our usual means of knowledge, as we do with any other object. This difficulty makes the project of trying to get to know the knower within us seem a bit nebulous and dubious. However, we should bear in mind that, at the initial stage, we do not really need iron-clad proof that there is a real self but only a reasonable basis for commencing our inquiry. Some initial haziness here should not put us off in our quest.

The second question we need to deal with is whether Vedanta is really the means of self-knowledge. If this question is asked *before* commencing to invest the effort and time needed to expose ourselves to the teachings of Vedanta, then perhaps the question could be answered by a counter-question: *Is there any way of proving to ourselves the efficacy of any means of knowledge except by suitably employing that means?* A little story, used by a well-known teacher of Vedanta, may make this clearer. This story is about a person who unfortunately has been born blind and has grown up to be an adult without ever being able to employ one of our most important means of knowledge: sight perception. Many doctors have examined this person in the past and the conclusion so far has been that he suffers from a type of optical nerve defect which is not amenable to any known treatment. With progress in medical research and technology, the happy day dawns when a new surgical procedure is perfected that is likely to work for our man's problem. Surgery is duly carried out, and the patient's eyes are bandaged to aid healing. The doctors are happy with the way the surgery has gone and there have been no post-operative complications. Finally, the time comes when the bandages covering the eyes are removed. The doctors now ask this person to gently open his eyes, and everyone waits with bated breath to see the reaction of a man using the wonderful gift of sight for the first time. At this stage the patient diffidently says, "I have been blind all my life and I have come to terms with my blindness. I can deal with blindness. I cannot deal with the hope of being able to see, only to find, with crushing disappointment, that the surgery did not work in my case. I have, therefore, decided not to open my eyes till you can prove to me that I will really be able to see when I do open my eyes!"

What can be done in this situation? Can any total proof be provided here? This cannot be done, because each separate means of knowledge is only self-proving and can never be fully established by any other means of knowledge. The final proof of the existence of the faculty of sight can only be in actually seeing, that is, by employing that faculty. Vedanta is an independent means of knowledge. We can look upon its long history and consider the experiences of many others who have benefited from Vedanta; these can be only tentative reasons for believing that Vedanta is likely to work for us as well. The ultimate proof can lie only in us actually employing this means of knowledge ourselves, and this can be done only by exposing ourselves to the teachings of Vedanta. Unfortunately, here the issue is not as simple as opening our eyelids. For Vedanta to work as a means of knowledge, we need adequate preparedness and the help of an appropriate teacher. Much effort and good fortune are required here.

Doubts about Vedanta really being the appropriate means of self-knowledge can also be raised *after* some exposure to Vedanta teachings. The reasons here could be different from the reasons which come up when such doubts are raised prior to study. Very often there is frustration and impatience when Vedanta does not appear to be delivering on its promise in quick order. After all, as soon as anyone has read or heard the words *tat tvam asi* or *You are That*, that person has been actually exposed to the core of Vedanta's teachings. However, these words do not make any real difference to what we understand, or in what we feel and do.

This does not mean that the teachings of Vedanta do not work. We, first of all, have to assess and work on our own qualifications or preparedness for such teachings. Even then, we will not benefit from Vedanta's words beyond a point unless these words are skillfully wielded and systematically unfolded by a fully qualified teacher. Finally, we must recognize the need for time in this sort of learning. Our notions of who we are have been built up over a long time and have gone in very deep. Initially, when we are told that we are different from who or what we think we are, this is just treated as another bit of information by the mind. This new information becomes one more layer of conditioning on top of what we think we are. The ego's natural reaction is to use this new information for strengthening itself, while the real need is for the ego to subside! This new understanding has to percolate and settle so that it does not become fresh ammunition for the ego to use in its battles but instead becomes a means of knowing that *there is really no battle at all for the real self*. This is a subtle and time-consuming process for most of us. Both understanding and patience are required for Vedanta to prove itself as the means for self-knowledge, and in the interim some faith is indispensable.

What is the merit or purpose of self-knowledge? This is the third and last question we posed for ourselves, and this question can be answered from several perspectives. Let us begin with the consequence of self-ignorance. The problem here does not stop at merely self-ignorance but gets converted into a problem of wrong notions and false conclusions. When we fail to shed ignorance of our true nature, we never come to the conclusion that "I do not know who I am or what I am." We, in fact, come to the *wrong* conclusion that "I am my body and my mind" (or some sort of a combination thereof). This conclusion, in turn, makes the limitations of the body and the mind into *our* limitations. Our body and mind are limited in their capacity to exist, to know, and to be happy because all bodies and minds will die, and that too without knowing everything and without being always happy. By looking upon our body and mind as our true self, we convert our life into an endeavor to overcome these limitations. This effort is ceaseless and can never be ultimately successful because the limitations we try to overcome are an inherent part of our body and mind. Depending upon our mental make-up, for many of us this attempt becomes a frantic, ego-driven struggle which robs our life of simple peace and contentment.

We must clearly understand here that the problem is not in the general tendency of human beings to try to overcome the limitations of their body and mind; such a tendency is an inherent part of human beings. The problem of self-ignorance is that by limiting our understanding of our own self as being *only* our body and mind, we take a different type of personal delivery of the natural struggle to overcome body-mind limitations. We then look upon the results of this struggle as the sole determinant of our happiness as well as the definition of our success. All this, of course, happens at the level of the ego, and in this context the purpose of knowing and understanding our real nature is to stop us from being in a constantly antagonistic state with the rest of the world, which comes from living only at the ego's level. We need to get off a treadmill going nowhere not because we are on the wrong treadmill or because we are not running fast enough but because treadmills of the body and mind just cannot ever take the real us anywhere.

The other way to look at the need for self-knowledge is in the light of our own experience of growth. To grow in several facets does not seem to be a matter of choice for human beings. Physical growth occurs as a result of nutrition and the efflux of time; beyond a certain level, emotional and intellectual growth seems to require our willful effort, but the urge to grow itself springs spontaneously from within us. In fact, stagnation is not compatible with life—we cannot be static for any length of time without the consequence of atrophy. The urge to fight stasis and atrophy, by growth, is built into us. Our inherent urge to grow naturally takes us in the direction of overcoming our perceived limitations, because growth carries the connotation of freedom. We are all instinctively led to efforts to perpetuate our existence, to know more, and to be happy; in other words, to be free of the basic limitations of mortality, ignorance, and unhappiness. Depending upon our physical and mental qualities, these efforts can be intense, awesome, wonderful in their scope and beauty, and of great use to the rest of humankind.

However, no matter how mighty our efforts to grow, they make no real dent in the fundamental sense of limitation which comes from taking a limited body and a limited mind as our true self. Without proper understanding of our real nature, the frustrated efforts to overcome our notion of limitation drives some of us to push ourselves to higher and more precarious levels. All these efforts lead only to finite and temporal results which can never fully satisfy. If we do not understand this, then we can end up making more efforts, seeking more possessions, needing higher levels of risk and excitement, and having greater hopes that the next possession/project/relationship will do the trick of bringing lasting fulfillment and freedom to us. However, these things are only crutches, and total freedom can never be achieved by acquiring bigger, better, and more beautiful crutches. We may then console ourselves by saying that ceaseless striving is the only way to live life and by claiming that being a perpetual seeker is great fun. In fact, many of us actually end up getting angry, tired, depressed, scared, and guilty; we may feel persecuted as well as look for scapegoats. In spite of all our achievements and possessions, a sense of real self-worth, a sense of inner wholesomeness and tranquility, seems to elude us.

The only solution for those of us in this situation is to redirect at least part of our energy, to grow in self-knowledge. Growth in this direction alone can ultimately solve our problem, not by stifling the growth instinct but by using it to grow up to be in full and objective touch with our own reality. And the reality is that we are not only a body and mind combination; we are much more than that, and therefore we need not feel limited or threatened by the limitations of our physical and mental adjuncts. Grow we must—but growth which does not include self-knowledge can never lead us to our full potential and our own truth. A life lived out of touch with our reality can become a tragedy and a waste; it can convert a wonderful opportunity for living and experiencing into a grim and tense battle, with only pride, guilt, and hostility as the main fruits. And the wonderful thing about Vedanta is that it starts making a very valuable difference to our internal equilibrium, and therefore to our quality of life, much before we fully imbibe its final teachings. Some of the initial thinking and the preparatory teachings of Vedanta themselves bring about a very significant change in the understanding of our own motivations and emotions as well as of those around us. Better understanding of these matters, and a more sensible relationship with an acceptable concept of God, permits proper processing of our emotions as well as of several matters buried in our subconscious. This is both a healing and nurturing process and provides us with inner space and an inner sense of leisure, hitherto unknown to many of us.

But what about those of us who are in comfortable equilibrium with life and living, who do not feel particularly limited by our body and mind, and who are not too curious to know about any "real self"? After all, many of us are quite content to do whatever we can without making life into a painful struggle. Why should such people bother about Vedanta? Let me begin by saying that I sincerely salute those who *really* abide in this peaceful state for their ability and good sense in managing their emotions and desires so well. I also hope that they realize what a debt of gratitude they owe to God, destiny, or their past karmas for this happy state. I would yet like to point out two different reasons which one should consider before deciding not to look at what Vedanta has to offer.

The first and the more obvious reason is that there can, of course, never be any guarantee that such a wonderful situation will last forever. Change is the very basis of life and nobody knows what the next year or the next day or even the next moment will bring. While our record of balanced responses to change in the past should certainly provide some comfort while facing an unknown future, it is impossible to predict when a major change in our external or internal environment may bring about a fall from our current equilibrium. Vedanta points to equilibrium based on the knowledge of our true self—which is not only beyond our external surroundings but also beyond our mind, wherein experiences of happiness and unhappiness arise. Equilibrium of this nature has to be fundamental and must remain unaffected by any change. It would seem to me that if one is currently in a state wherein the body and mind are reasonably balanced and contented, this should be looked upon as a blessing and an opportunity to build a further and more basic capability to deal with future changes. Any teaching which is to put us in touch with our unchanging real nature should be of vital importance here and must merit serious examination.

Let us look at another argument, which though a bit more involved, yet goes to show that even the more fortunate and the more contented amongst us should consider Vedanta's teachings. When we, as human beings, look upon all other types of living creatures on this planet, we do recognize ourselves as a different and dominant species. We certainly are not amongst the oldest inhabitants of earth, nor do we boast of unsurpassed muscular strength or of exceptional acuity of our physical senses. What, then, is special or different about human beings compared to other animals? The answer lies in the different and larger development of our brains (more specifically, of the frontal lobes) *and* a distinctive sense of self-consciousness which no other animal appears to share with us. These attributes equip us to do amazingly complex thinking and to experience a variety of emotions; they also make us capable of judging ourselves via the ego, which exists as a special sense of individuality and free will.

All these attributes are endowments or privileges which we uniquely enjoy as human beings. To have the thinking power of human beings is special, and to be self-aware of one's individual identity is also special. It seems to be a waste of our potential if we do not put these two special attributes together to think about and fully understand our apparent individuality and examine whether there is any more substance to us beyond our obvious composition. After all, we continuously use our special faculties in a wonderful and useful voyage of discovery of the external world, which extends to distant planets and galaxies; our own mind and body too are external in the sense that they are also objects of our cognition and understanding. As far as I am concerned, it would be very difficult to logically justify not turning a part of that curiosity and effort inwards to examine our real essence, which supports the body and the mind.

But is it valid to argue that we should make an effort to know our own real self just because it is there? To some extent the argument that one should use one's special attributes "because they are there" may seem like the mountaineer's rationale for climbing mountains. However, there is a very big difference. There is obviously a limit to the number of things we can do, experience, or learn about. One has to use good sense to decide what to take interest in and what to ignore. If we choose not to climb a mountain, pass up some kind of experience, or ignore some specific knowledge out of the mass of conventional knowledge which is available, then that is not only fine but is, in fact, a practical necessity. But when the subject on which we have to sit in judgment is self-knowledge, we have an obvious and fundamental difficulty. It again comes back to the impossibility of using our usual faculties and discrimination to evaluate anything connected with our very substratum, from which our faculties and discrimination themselves arise. So, when we say "I do not want to pursue Vedanta," who is actually saying this? Vedanta says that all our thinking, judging, and deciding is at the level of the mind, which includes emotions, intellect, and the ego; Vedanta further says that our true self is beyond the mind and it cannot be known except by using a completely different and unique means of knowledge, which is what Vedanta is.

If Vedanta is rejected prior to self-knowledge, then two things are clear. The first is that something has been rejected without any real basis for judgment, because all our other experiences, knowledge, and faculties do not in any way equip us to make any judgment about the existence or utility of the real *I*. The second fact is that the decision to ignore Vedanta can come only from that self which, Vedanta says, is not our true self. Logically, therefore, Vedanta can never be justifiably rejected by our true self without full and proper pursuit of Vedanta itself! Until we actually complete our pursuit of Vedanta, our real and true self will remain covered and misunderstood and we cannot know what we are shutting out.

Do these various arguments for Vedanta mean that all people have to or should or will pursue this knowledge? The fact is that very few people at any time and in any age have had the inclination to undertake a serious pursuit of Vedanta.[40] That this has been so and will be so is recognized by Vedanta itself. Vedantic tradition has, in fact, been against general dissemination of this knowledge. This is based on the fact that if a seeker is not duly qualified, the teachings of Vedanta will not only be ineffective but can also be harmful, either in terms of encouraging perverse thinking or by causing a breakdown of an individual's comforting infrastructure of beliefs and conditioning.

Therefore a duty is cast upon a knower or teacher to make a very careful assessment of a seeker's preparedness and capability before launching the seeker into the open waters of Vedanta in its full scope (though, of course, everybody can benefit from the more protected waters of Vedanta's initial and preparatory teachings). Leaving aside Vedanta's own safeguards, we have to recognize that no

---

40. What is meant here by *Vedanta* is any means of obtaining true knowledge of our self and achieving complete growth and freedom. Whether or not this effort is labeled *Vedanta* (and whether or not Sanskrit terminology is used) does not really matter. On the other hand, unless someone has adequate reason to hold strong convictions about some alternative means of knowledge, it would seem unnecessarily brave and risky here to bypass Vedanta, which has such tested and beautiful methods and traditions in this matter.

amount of persuasion and argument will convince some of us to expose ourselves to this knowledge. When a particular inclination or attitude towards a given topic is not present in an individual, that person has the capacity to rationalize and justify any decision they might make regarding that topic, no matter what. Further, even from amongst those who actually begin the pursuit of Vedanta, only a few will have the inclination and capacity to run the full course.

Where does all this lead us? What happens if we just cannot get interested enough in Vedanta to make it into a meaningful pursuit? What happens if even after pursuing Vedanta for some time, its teachings do not seem to take hold and work for us in our daily life? Looking at these problems from the impersonal (and seemingly harsh) viewpoint of the totality of creation, both our individual fate and the message of Vedanta are of no particular consequence. An individual's personal potential, problems, and agenda are not significant issues from that perspective. The scale and mystery of creation are immensely large and complex. On that scale, entire stellar systems come into being and are destroyed without any noticeable consequence, just as tiny grass flowers are born and die unnoticed in our forests. In terms of the history of this tiny planet alone, the human race has been in existence for a length of time which could be spoken of as the twinkling of an eye. In another twinkling of an eye our entire race could be wiped out and become a historical footnote as an interesting (and perhaps dangerous) experiment in the manifestation of consciousness. On their own time scale, our planet and the universe will be undisturbed in their own path, irrespective of our doings. We need to be aware of our own reality, not as pinnacles of creation weighed down by a heavy sense of cosmic responsibility but as individuals who need to solve their own problems of finding meaning and of living in happiness. This solution can ultimately come from knowing and understanding our own selves. If we cannot or do not make this effort, only we as individuals will be losers and nothing else will be affected.

In the ultimate analysis one can only say that, like everything else, the inability or unwillingness to grow in this direction has also to be part of the scheme of creation, which must be unfolding as it should. Each life has to be lived and dealt with as it unfolds in its own way. There is no doubt that many human lives have been and will continue to be spent in pursuits which apparently do not contribute to any self-knowledge; I have no doubt that this happens because that is the way it is supposed to be. Beyond a point, one need not read anything individual or personal into all this. While there are good reasons to try to apply ourselves with diligence and fervor to the task of gaining self-knowledge, we must temper our endeavors and aspirations with humility coming from the understanding that our choices and the results of our actions depend upon a whole host of factors (we can call them fate, circumstances, God's grace, luck, or whatever else we may like), many of which are beyond our control and even beyond our knowledge. To turn to Vedanta to find an answer to our sense of limitation and then to let Vedanta become a source of further complexes, which increase our sense of inadequacy or limitation, would really be a cruel case of jumping from the proverbial frying pan into the fire. One can only pray, in the words of this well-known prayer:

God give me the courage to change the things I can,
the serenity to accept the things I cannot,
and the wisdom to know the difference.

and understand, as we pray, that there is no guarantee that the required wisdom will necessarily be available to us.

On a more positive note, the very fact that we have taken any interest at all in a subject like Vedanta goes to show that a certain amount of good fortune is already working for us. Even casual interest in Vedanta very often provides an opportunity to examine the framework of our usual understanding and efforts. If this interest can be sustained, if it gets further encouragement from association with good people and useful books, and if the blessing of finding a real teacher happens to us, then we are truly hooked—our weaknesses and past conditioning may hold us back and make us struggle, but in the long run they cannot keep us away from our destiny of freedom by self-knowledge. So with faith and effort, let us persevere in our attempts to share the vision of the seers recorded in the Upanishads and, in the process, enjoy the journey of life and learning. Let us end with a prayer from the Upanishads:

asatoma sadgamaya
tamasoma jyotirgamaya
mrityorma amritamgamaya
om shanti shanti shantih

From untruth, lead me to truth.
From darkness, lead me to light.
From mortality, lead me to immortality.
May there be peace in all aspects of life.

Acknowledgments

———————◆———————

Hindu dharma scriptures say that each human being has five debts which he has to recognize and discharge. These debts are:

1. To *rishis*, who were sages and the unknown authors of the Vedas, whose wisdom is available to us through our own teachers.

I have been blessed in having the benefit of the knowledge, wisdom, compassion, and love of more than one great teacher. Anything in this book which is true I have learnt with their grace; all I have done is to paraphrase their teachings into my own words. However, I am not acknowledging these teachers by name, for two main reasons. The first is that I would like to claim originality for all errors and wrong understanding—these are, of course, entirely mine! The second reason is that tradition says that the debt to rishis can be fully settled only by studying and understanding their teachings properly. I hope I will be able to fulfill my duty in this matter by walking further along the path of learning which they have so brilliantly and lovingly shown to me.

2. To *pitrs*, ancestors, without whom we would not have been born and whose nurture and guidance have been essential for us.

My indebtedness to my lineage and specially to my parents is, of course, boundless. Apart from my very existence, I am grateful to my parents for the values and attitudes which they imparted and the love for learning in all areas which they instilled. Tradition says that to serve your parents is the way to repay this debt. As both my parents have passed away, I can only hope that I was of some service to them during their lifetimes and that I can live up to at least a few of the ideals that they stood for.

3. To *devas*, the various gods representing individual forces of nature.

We can only be grateful for the natural order and for the resources, with which we all have been provided, to not only live but to enjoy living. The gods have been truly kind. I try to acknowledge this debt by a continuing sense of interconnection with nature in all its different facets as well as by regular prayer to express humility and gratitude.

4. To *bhu*—that is, or to all other life-forms and objects in this world.

Here, the point is to recognize our dependence on animals, birds, insects, plants, and all things on this earth in general. Apart from recognizing these as fortunate gifts, one needs to develop a caring mindfulness in dealing with them. To the extent we must use nature's resources, this should be done without an arrogant or an exploitative attitude.

5. To *nara*, human beings, because as individuals we exist in special relationship with other human beings.

As a way of honoring this debt, traditional scriptures provide a whole set of norms to be followed in dealing with other human beings. An instance of such a norm is the concept of *atithi dharma*, which is an obligation to welcome and provide for each and every guest who comes to one's home (even if the guest is an unpleasant or an inimical person).

On a more personal plane, and in the context of this book, I would like to express my sincere appreciation to my family and several friends who have patiently suffered me and my aberrations in my attempts to learn something of Vedanta as well as in the effort to write this book.

An immense amount of gratitude goes to my friend,

Raghu, who has not only been a wonderful companion in the study of Vedanta for the last several years but has also greatly contributed to all aspects of this book with his learning, objectivity, and encouragement.

I am also indebted to several efficient and helpful people who have compensated for my lack of computer skills by deciphering large quantities of atrocious handwriting and putting all the material through word-processing programs.

Finally, I would like to express special gratitude to any reader of this book. Without the prospect of readers, I would not have attempted such a book and would have missed out on the great deal of learning which the process of writing this book has brought to me, apart from the joy I have had in writing. I do hope that, in return, this book provides its readers with something of value and interest.

Some Interesting Books

IT IS A BIT DIFFICULT to recommend books connected with Vedanta, given the nature of the subject. Interpretations in different books are often contradictory, and some are actually misleading in parts; the difficulty with translations is even greater, because they inevitably bear the imprint of the translator's orientation and intention. What follows, therefore, is simply a list of some books which I have personally found interesting and useful, at times only in portions. One important common feature in them, of course, is that they are all in English, though many of them also contain the appropriate Sanskrit text.

TRADITIONAL ADVAITA VEDANTA BOOKS
1. *Eight Upanishads* [in two volumes] – Swami Gambhirananda.
   Advaita Ashrama, Calcutta
Translation of eight of the ten principal Upanishads along with Shankara's commentary. For a beginner, only the translation of the text of the Upanishads can be read initially; the commentary can be gone into on a subsequent reading. The portion containing the *Mandukya Upanishad* also includes Gaudapada's *karika*, which sets out some of the most far-reaching conclusions of advaita Vedanta.

2. *The Principal Upanishads* – Sri Swami Sivananda.
   Divine Life Society, Shivanandanagar, Uttar Pradesh, India
Translation of eight important Upanishads in a concise volume with notes and brief commentary.

3. *Upadesa Sahasri* – V. Narasimhan.
   Bharatiya Vidya Bhavan, Bombay
Translation (with commentary) of a *prakarana* work—
the only one if its kind accepted by modern scholars as
being undoubtedly Shankara's.

4. *The Quintessence of Vedanta* – Swami Tattwananda.
   Sri Ramakrishna Advaita Ashram, Kerala, India
Bare translation of one of Shankara's relatively obscure
works, which sets out many important aspects of Vedanta
in a rather precise and structured manner.

5. *Vakyavritti and Atmajñanopadeshavidhi* – Swami
   Jagadananda.
   Sri Ramakrishna Math, Madras, India
Translation (with a few notes) of two more concise,
introductory Vedanta books of Shankara in a single, small
volume.

6. *Vivekachudamani* – English translation by P.
   Sankaranarayanan of the Sanskrit work by
   Chandrasekhara Bharati, the Sringeri
   Shankaracharya.
   Bharatiya Vidya Bhavan, Bombay
Translation (with commentary) of this large and well-
known work of Shankara which forms the basis of a rather
comprehensive introduction to Vedanta for many serious
students.

7. *Atma Bodha* [Self-Knowledge] – Swami Nikhilananda.
   Sri Ramakrishna Math, Madras, India
Translation (with commentary) of Shankara's concise,
introductory book which is often used as the basis for
initial, short courses on Vedanta. This book also contains a
rather elaborate but useful introduction to Vedanta and
ends with several songs of praise and hymns attributed to
Shankara.

8. *Astavakragita* – Radhakamal Mukerjee.
   Motilal Banarsidass, New Delhi
Translation (with commentary) of this beautiful text in
the form of a dialogue between the realized teacher
Astavakra and his brilliant pupil, the ancient king Janaka.

9. *Introduction to Vedanta* – Swami Dayananda.
   Vision Books, New Delhi
A concise but effective introduction which outlines the
fundamental human problem in a simple manner but in
keeping with Vedanta's highest traditions.

10. *Bhagavad Gita* – Swami Gambhirananda.
    Advaita Ashrama, Calcutta
Scholarly translation with Shankara's commentary.

11. *Bhagavad Gita Home Study Program* – Swami
    Dayananda.
    Arsha Vidya Gurukulam, Coimbatore, India
An exceptional resource for prolonged self-study at
home. 1,800 pages based on a series of 400 lectures. The
next best thing to going to a traditional teacher.

12. *The Teaching of the Bhagavad Gita* – Swami
    Dayananda.
    Vision Books, New Delhi
A brief and lucid introduction to the teachings of the
Bhagavad Gita, drawing upon its key verses.

OTHER VEDANTA BOOKS
1. *The Upanishads* – Eknath Easwaran, ed.
   Nilgiri Press, Tomales, Calif.
Translation of several Upanishads (some only in part),
including a few of the so-called "minor" Upanishads, along

with notes and excellent introductions and afterword. Written with poetry and feeling.

2. *From the Upanishads* – Ananda Wood.
   Full Circle, 18–19 Dilshad Garden, G.T. Road, Delhi 110 095

A refreshing "re-telling" of passages from several Upanishads; not a simple translation, but an innovative interpretation.

3. *Be As You Are: The Teachings of Sri Ramana Maharshi* – David Godman, ed.
   Arkana [Penguin Books], London

A collection of excerpts from conversations between one of the most significant saints of twentieth-century India and the many seekers who visited him. This concise but valuable book contains the essence of his teachings, arranged by the compiler in different sections with separate introductory notes.

4. *I Am That: Talks with Sri Nisargadatta Maharaj* – Maurice Frydman, trans.
   Acorn Press, Durham, N.C.

Another collection of question and answer sessions with a sage of our times; a book which has spurred many modern people, from a variety of backgrounds, to explore advaita Vedanta.

5. *Final Truth: A Guide to Ultimate Understanding* – Ramesh S. Balsekar.
   Advaita Press, Redondo Beach, Calif.

A stimulating book based on deep learning and experience by the contemporary torchbearer of Nisargadatta Maharaj's teachings of pure advaita.

6. *Vedanta: Heart of Hinduism* – German original by Hans Torwesten, adapted by Loly Rosset from John Phillips' translation.
Grove Press, New York City
Unique and thought-provoking book which not only provides a concise and intelligent overview but also relates major ideas to Western thought.

NON-VEDANTA BOOKS

1. *The Heart of Buddhism* – Guy Claxton.
Thorsons [HarperCollins], London
Very readable and valuable not only for what it has to say about Buddhism but also about our ways of thinking and behavior.

2. *What Does It All Mean?* – Thomas Nagel.
Oxford University Press, New York City
Very short introduction to some perennial questions we ask about ourselves. The brief discussion within the format of Western philosophy is thoughtful and clear.

3. *The Tao of Physics* – Fritjof Capra.
Bantam Books, New York City
A New Age book from the 1970s—a bestseller which analyzes texts from Hinduism, Buddhism, and Taoism to show striking parallels with scientific discoveries of the present century.

4. *The Conquest of Happiness* – Bertrand Russell.
W. W. Norton, New York City
A simple but valuable approach containing practical common sense from this well-known philosopher.

5. *The Road Less Traveled* – M. Scott Peck.
Simon & Schuster, New York City
A very helpful book from a practicing psychiatrist

dealing with behavior and attitudes which have an impact on mental and spiritual growth.

6. *The Wisdom of Insecurity* – Alan Watts.
   Random House, London

An interesting exploration of the propositions, in the spirit of Taoism, that insecurity is the result of trying to be secure and that salvation consists in the radical recognition that we have no way of saving ourselves.

7. *Philosophy: A Beginner's Guide* – Jenny Teichman & Katherine C. Evans.
   Blackwell Publishers, Oxford

A non-intimidating, clear, and informative introduction to the main aspects of Western philosophy.

Glossary

———◆———

adhikari   one qualified (for self-knowledge)

adhikaritvam   eligibility (for studying Vedanta)

adrishta phala   invisible and indirect result

advaita   non-dual

advaita Vedanta   non-dual view of reality derived from the Upanishads and elaborated into a system of philosophy

agami   newly gathered karma

ahimsa   abstaining from killing or from harming others in thought, word, or deed

ananda   a state of happiness born out of fullness or completeness; the third component of the compound *sat-chit-ananda*

ananta   limitless

anantam   limitlessness

anitya   time-bound

artha   objective; security (economic, physical, or emotional); wealth

ashram   hermitage or community home led by a guru; stage of life

atma   the true self, which is not different from brahman; innermost essence of the human being unfolded by Vedanta, the definition or nature of which is *sat-chit-ananda*: timeless existence, self-evident consciousness, and limitlessness

bhakti   worship, love, devotion (in relation to a personal god)

bhashya   commentary (on a prime Vedantic text)

bhikshu   person who lives on alms; Buddhist monk

brahmacharya being a student—the first of the four stages of traditional life in Vedic times

brahman non-dual fundamental reality which is the truth of everything

brahmanishtha one who is established in or committed to brahman

Brahma Sutras concise and logically arranged aphorisms written by Badarayana containing the essence of the Upanishads; one of the three starting points of Vedantic philosophy

chit self-evident consciousness or awareness; the second component of the compound *sat-chit-ananda*

dharma righteousness, propriety, virtue, duty

drishta phala visible and direct result

grihastha householder—the second stage of traditional life in Vedic times

guru remover of darkness (teacher of self-knowledge)

jijñasu seeker of knowledge (to dispel self-ignorance)

jñana knowledge (usually denotes insight or direct knowledge of reality)

jñani person who has complete and permanent self-knowledge

kama pleasures (physical, emotional, or aesthetic)

karma action based on free will; results of actions

karma (theory of) theory of causality stating that all actions lead not only to direct and visible results but also to indirect and invisible results

karma phala result of any action

karma yoga leading a normal, ethical life with the goal of *moksha*, wherein actions are undertaken with a certain objective attitude towards results

kriyamana newly gathered karma

mahavakya great sentence (which reveals the self)

mantra verbal expression which may be a syllable, word,

phrase, or verse used for recitation, chanting, or meditation—oral or mental

mithya   that which has a dependent existence

moksha   liberation from the sense of limitation in general

mumukshu   seeker with a burning desire for liberation

mumukshutvam   state of having a burning desire for liberation

nitya   eternal, constant

papa   invisible or indirect results of wrong or prohibited actions

prakarana   treatise expounding on a given topic or on a facet of a topic

prakriya   method of unfoldment or exposition

pramana   means of knowledge

prarabdha   results of past actions (of earlier births) accounting for this birth and to be exhausted in this lifetime

prasada   gift of God; the portion of a consecrated offering returned to worshippers

punya   invisible or indirect results of actions in accordance with righteousness

purushartha   principal objectives of a human life

sanchita   accumulated results of all actions (of present and past births) not exhausted in this lifetime

sannyasa   renunciation, a life committed to knowledge and free of other roles; the fourth stage of traditional life in Vedic times

sannyasin   person having adopted a life of *sannyasa*

sat   timeless, limitless existence (the first component of the compound *sat-chit-ananda*)

satyam   that which exists; the nature of truth

shabda pramana   words as a means of knowledge

shloka   verse

shrotriya   one who is well-versed in the scriptures

shruti   that which was heard (i.e., revealed); the summary designation of the Hindu scriptures which have the status of a divine revelation

smriti   memory; a category of Hindu scriptures recognized as human compositions

sukshma sharira   subtle body

tuchham   that which does not exist

Upanishads   philosophical portions found at the end of the four Vedas and collectively also called Vedanta; a unique means of self-knowledge

vanaprastha   state of withdrawal from work and family life; the third stage of traditional life in Vedic times

Veda(s)   a compilation of that which is known; a summary name for four sacred scriptures of Hinduism regarded as divine revelation

Vedanta   collective name for the philosophical portions found at the end of the four Vedas; also, a school of philosophy which accepts the authority of the Vedas, with special emphasis on the contents of the Upanishads

Vedic   prescribed by or in conformity with the Vedas

viveka   discrimination (between the eternal and the time-bound)

viveki   one who has discrimination (between the eternal and the time-bound)

yoga   to unite or yoke; a means for accomplishing something; one of the six traditional schools of Indian philosophy

About the Author

♦

DHRUV S. KAJI was born in India but spent most of his childhood in eastern Africa. He returned to India to complete his education, then entered the corporate world as a chartered accountant. He served as finance director for a large group of manufacturing companies, but eventually left this position in search of more meaningful pursuits. After a period without any real direction spent experimenting with white-water rafting, skydiving, acrobatic flying, and other adventure sports, he discovered Vedanta. He has been studying Vedanta since 1990 with swamis, university professors, and other teachers, both traditional and nontraditional. He now lives in Bombay and Singapore with his wife and two children, where he continues his study of Vedanta while working as a management consultant.

The main building of the Institute headquarters, near Honesdale, Pennsylvania.

The Himalayan Institute

FOUNDED IN 1971 by Swami Rama, the Himalayan Institute has been dedicated to helping people grow physically, mentally, and spiritually by combining the best knowledge of both the East and the West.

Our international headquarters is located on a beautiful 400-acre campus in the rolling hills of the Pocono Mountains of northeastern Pennsylvania. The atmosphere here is one to foster growth, increased inner awareness, and calm. Our grounds provide a wonderfully peaceful and healthy setting for our seminars and extended programs. Students from around the world join us here to attend programs in such diverse areas as hatha yoga, meditation, stress reduction, Ayurveda, nutrition, Eastern philosophy, psychology, and other subjects. Whether the programs are for weekend meditation retreats, week-long seminars on spirituality, months-long residential programs, or holistic health services, the attempt here is to provide an environment of gentle inner progress. We invite you to join with us in the ongoing process of personal growth and development.

The Institute is a nonprofit organization. Your membership in the Institute helps to support its programs. Please call or write for information on becoming a member.

Institute Programs, Services, and Facilities

Institute programs share an emphasis on conscious holistic living and personal self-development, including:

Special weekend or extended seminars to teach skills and techniques for increasing your ability to be healthy and enjoy life

Meditation retreats and advanced meditation and philosophical instruction

Vegetarian cooking and nutritional training

Hatha yoga and exercise workshops

Residential programs for self-development

Holistic health services and Ayurvedic Rejuvenation Programs through the Institute's Center for Health and Healing.

A *Quarterly Guide to Programs and Other Offerings* is free within the USA. To request a copy, or for further information, call 800-822-4547 or 570-253-5551, fax 570-253-9078, email bqinfo@himalayaninstitute.org, write the Himalayan Institute, RR 1 Box 400, Honesdale, PA 18431-9706 USA, or visit our website at www. himalayaninstitute.org.

The Himalayan Institute Press

THE HIMALAYAN INSTITUTE PRESS has long been regarded as "The Resource for Holistic Living." We publish dozens of titles, as well as audio and video tapes, that offer practical methods for living harmoniously and achieving inner balance. Our approach addresses the whole person—body, mind, and spirit—integrating the latest scientific knowledge with ancient healing and self-development techniques.

As such, we offer a wide array of titles on physical and psychological health and well-being, spiritual growth through meditation and other yogic practices, as well as translations of yogic scriptures.

Our sidelines include the Japa Kit for meditation practice, the Neti™ Pot, the ideal tool for sinus and allergy sufferers, and The Breath Pillow,™ a unique tool for learning health-supportive diaphragmatic breathing.

Subscriptions are available to a bimonthly magazine, *Yoga International,* which offers thought-provoking articles on all aspects of meditation and yoga, including yoga's sister science, Ayurveda.

For a free catalog call 800-822-4547 or 570-253-5551, email hibooks@himalayaninstitute.org, fax 570-253-6360, write the Himalayan Institute Press, RR 1 Box 405, Honesdale, PA 18431-9709, USA, or visit our website at www.himalayaninstitute.org.